Foundation
MATHEMATICS
for Edexcel GCSE

Tony Banks and David Alcorn

Causeway Press

Pearson Education Limited
Edinburgh Gate
Harlow
Essex
CM20 2JE
England

© Tony Banks and David Alcorn, 2007

The rights of Tony Banks and David Alcorn to be identified as the authors of this work have been asserted by them in accordance with the Copyright, Designs and Patents Act, 1988.

All rights reserved. No part of this publication may be reproduced, stored in a retrieval system, or transmitted in any form or by any means, electronic, mechanic, photocopying, recording, or otherwise, without either the prior written permission of the Publishers or a licence permitting restricted copying in the United Kingdom issued by the
Copyright Licensing Agency Ltd, 90 Tottenham Court Road, London W1P 9HE.

ISBN-13: 978-1-4058-3499-5
ISBN-10: 1-4058-3498-4

Endorsement
This high quality material is endorsed by Edexcel and has been through a rigorous quality assurance programme to ensure that it is a suitable companion to the specification for both learners and teachers. This does not mean that its contents will be used verbatim when setting examinations, nor is it to be read as being the official specification - a copy of which is available at   www.edexcel.org.uk

Exam questions
Past exam questions, provided by *London Examinations, a division of Edexcel*, are marked Edexcel. The answers to all questions are entirely the responsibility of the authors/publisher and have neither been provided nor approved by Edexcel.

Every effort has been made to locate the copyright owners of material used in this book. Any omissions brought to the notice of the publisher are regretted and will be credited in subsequent printings.

Page design
Billy Johnson

Reader
Barbara Alcorn

Artwork
David Alcorn

Cover design
Raven Design

Typesetting by Billy Johnson, San Francisco, California, USA

Printed and bound by Scotprint, Haddington, Scotland

preface

This book provides detailed revision notes, worked examples and examination questions to support students in their preparation for the new two-tier GCSE Mathematics examinations for the Edexcel Specifications – Foundation Tier.

The book has been designed so that it can be used in conjunction with the companion book *Foundation Mathematics for Edexcel GCSE* or as a stand-alone revision book for self study and provides full coverage of the new Edexcel Specifications for the Foundation Tier of entry.

In preparing the text, full account has been made of the requirements for students to be able to use and apply mathematics in written examination papers and be able to solve problems in mathematics both with and without a calculator.

The detailed revision notes, worked examples and examination questions have been organised into 40 self-contained sections which meet the requirements of the National Curriculum and provide efficient coverage of the specifications.

Sections   1 - 11   Number
Sections 12 - 20   Algebra
Sections 21 - 33   Shape, Space and Measures
Sections 34 - 40   Handling Data

At the end of the sections on Number, Algebra, Shape, Space and Measures and Handling Data, section reviews are provided to give further opportunities to consolidate skills.

At the end of the book there is a final examination questions section with a further compilation of exam and exam-style questions, organised for non-calculator and calculator practice, in preparation for the exams.

Also available *Without Answers: (ISBN: 1-405834-98-6)*
The book has been designed so that it can be used in conjunction with the companion book
Foundation Mathematics for Edexcel GCSE (ISBN: 1-405831-40-5)

contents

Number Sections 1 - 11

1	Whole Numbers	1
2	Decimals	3
3	Approximation and Estimation	5
4	Negative Numbers	8
5	Fractions	10
6	Working with Number	12
7	Percentages	15
8	Time and Money	17
9	Personal Finance	19
10	Ratio and Proportion	21
11	Speed and Other Compound Measures	23

Section Review - Number

Non-calculator Paper ... 25
Calculator Paper ... 28

Algebra Sections 12 - 20

12	Introduction to Algebra	31
13	Solving Equations	33
14	Further Equations	34
15	Formulae	36
16	Sequences	38
17	Coordinates and Graphs	40
18	Using Graphs	42
19	Inequalities	45
20	Quadratic Graphs	46

Section Review - Algebra

Non-calculator Paper ... 47
Calculator Paper ... 50

Shape, Space and Measures   Sections 21 - 33

21	Angles	53
22	Triangles	55
23	Symmetry and Congruence	57
24	Quadrilaterals	59
25	Polygons	61
26	Direction and Distance	63
27	Circles	65
28	Areas and Volumes	67
29	Loci and Constructions	71
30	Transformations	73
31	Enlargements and Similar Figures	76
32	Pythagoras' Theorem	78
33	Understanding and Using Measures	80

Section Review - Shape, Space and Measures

Non-calculator Paper 82
Calculator Paper 85

Handling Data   Sections 34 - 40

34	Collection and Organisation of Data	88
35	Pictograms and Bar Charts	91
36	Averages and Range	93
37	Pie Charts and Stem and Leaf Diagrams	96
38	Time Series and Frequency Diagrams	98
39	Scatter Graphs	101
40	Probability	103

Section Review - Handling Data

Non-calculator Paper 106
Calculator Paper 109

Exam Practice

Non-calculator Paper 112
Calculator Paper 116

Answers 120

Index 136

SECTION 1  Whole Numbers

What you need to know

- You should be able to read and write numbers expressed in figures and words.

  Eg 1 The number 8543 is written or read as, "eight thousand five hundred and forty-three".

- Be able to order whole numbers.

  Eg 2 Write the numbers 17, 9, 35, 106 and 49 in ascending order.
  9, 17, 35, 49, 106

  Smallest number → ascending order → Largest number
  Largest number → descending order → Smallest number

- Be able to recognise the place value of each digit in a number.

  Eg 3 In the number 5384 the digit 8 is worth 80, but in the number 4853 the digit 8 is worth 800.

- Use mental methods to carry out addition and subtraction.
- Know the Multiplication Tables up to 10×10.
- Be able to: multiply whole numbers by 10, 100, 1000, …
  multiply whole numbers by 20, 30, 40, …
  divide whole numbers by 10, 100, 1000, …
  divide whole numbers by 20, 30, 40, …

×	1	2	3	4	5	6	7	8	9	10
1	1	2	3	4	5	6	7	8	9	10
2	2	4	6	8	10	12	14	16	18	20
3	3	6	9	12	15	18	21	24	27	30
4	4	8	12	16	20	24	28	32	36	40
5	5	10	15	20	25	30	35	40	45	50
6	6	12	18	24	30	36	42	48	54	60
7	7	14	21	28	35	42	49	56	63	70
8	8	16	24	32	40	48	56	64	72	80
9	9	18	27	36	45	54	63	72	81	90
10	10	20	30	40	50	60	70	80	90	100

Eg 4 Work out. (a) 75×100 (b) 42×30
$= 7500$ $= 42 \times 10 \times 3$
$= 420 \times 3$
$= 1260$

Eg 5 Work out. (a) $460 \div 10$ (b) $750 \div 30$
$= 46$ $= (750 \div 10) \div 3$
$= 75 \div 3$
$= 25$

- Use non-calculator methods for addition, subtraction, multiplication and division.

Eg 6 $476 + 254$
```
  4 7 6
+ 2 5 4
-------
  7 3 0
  1 1
```

Eg 7 $374 - 147$
```
  3 ⁶7̸ ¹4
-   1 4 7
---------
    2 2 7
```

Addition and Subtraction
Write the numbers in columns according to place value.
You can use addition to check your subtraction.

Eg 8 324×13
```
      3 2 4
   ×    1 3
  ---------
      9 7 2
  + 3 2 4 0
  ---------
    4 2 1 2
      1 1
```

Eg 9 $343 \div 7$
```
       4 9
   7)3 4 3
     2 8
     ---
       6 3
       6 3
       ---
         0
```

Long division
÷ (Obtain biggest answer possible.)
Calculate the remainder.
Bring down the next figure and repeat the process until there are no more figures to be brought down.

Long multiplication
Multiply by the units figure, then the tens figure, and so on. Then add these answers.

- Know the order of operations in a calculation.

First	Brackets and Division line
Second	Divide and Multiply
Third	Addition and Subtraction

  Eg 10 $4 + 2 \times 6 = 4 + 12 = 16$

  Eg 11 $9 \times (7 - 2) + 3 = 9 \times 5 + 3 = 45 + 3 = 48$

Exercise 1
Do not use a calculator for this exercise.

1 (a) Write **three hundred and fifty thousand** in figures.
   (b) (i) Write 25 400 in words. (ii) Write down the value of the **5** in 25 400. *Edexcel*

2 Write the numbers 85, 9, 23, 117 and 100 in order, largest first.

3 Here is a list of numbers. 3 5 8 9 11 14 15
From the numbers in the list, write down
   (a) a number which is even,
   (b) two numbers which have a sum of 25,
   (c) two numbers which have a difference of 7.

4 9 is the number that is halfway between 6 and 12.
Work out the number that is halfway between (a) 20 and 60, (b) 100 000 and 200 000. *Edexcel*

5 Write the number 60 000 000 in words.

6 Jamie buys these items at the school fair: cola 32p, sweets 45p, pencil 16p.
Find the total cost. *Edexcel*

7 (a) What must be added to 19 to make 100?
   (b) What are the missing values?
      (i) $100 - 65 = \square$ (ii) $12 \times \square = 1200$ (iii) $150 \div \square = 15$

8 Work out. (a) $769 + 236$ (b) $400 - 209$ (c) $258 - 75$

9 This table shows the numbers of jars of coffee sold in a shop.

	100 g	200 g	300 g	Total
Ground		50		120
Powder	80	35	26	
Granules	40	45		
Total	135		135	400

Copy and complete the table. *Edexcel*

10 (a) By using each of the digits 8, 5, 2 and 3, write down:
      (i) the smallest four-digit number,   (ii) the largest four-digit odd number.
   (b) What is the value of the 5 in the largest number?
   (c) What is the value of the 5 in the smallest number?
   (d) What is the difference between the two numbers you have written down in part (a)?

11 Work out. (a) 200×60 (b) $40\,000 \div 80$ (c) 25×7 (d) $45 \div 3$

12 (a) Find the missing numbers in these calculations.
      (i) $30 \div \square = 5$ (ii) $30 \times \square = 2400$ (iii) $\dfrac{6\,000\,000}{\square} = 30$

   (b) Complete this sentence. "When 300 is divided by 7, the remainder is ……."

13 Richard paid 56p for 7 pencils. The cost of each pencil was the same.
Work out the cost of 4 of these pencils. *Edexcel*

14 The chart shows the shortest distances, in kilometres, between pairs of cities.

London				
196	Nottingham			
300	101	Manchester		
325	158	56	Liverpool	
639	446	346	348	Glasgow

(a) Write down the shortest distance between **Nottingham** and **Liverpool**.
(b) Daniel drives from London to Manchester by the shortest route.
He has driven 137 km. Work out how many more kilometres he must drive.
(c) Write down the names of the two cities which are the **least** distance apart.

Edexcel

15 Last year Mr Alderton had the following household bills.

Gas	£364	Electricity	£158	Telephone	£187
Water	£244	Insurance	£236	Council Tax	£983

He paid the bills by 12 equal monthly payments.
How much was each monthly payment?

16 Petrol costs 89p per litre. Work out the cost of 12 litres.

Edexcel

17 A supermarket orders one thousand two hundred tins of beans.
The beans are sold in boxes of twenty-four.
How many boxes of beans are ordered?

18 Work out. (a) $6 + 4 \times 3$ (b) $96 \div (3 + 5)$ (c) $2 \times (18 - 12) \div 4$

19 Simon is 8 kg heavier than Matt. Their weights add up to 132 kg.
How heavy is Simon?

20 A roll of wire is 500 cm long. From the roll, Debra cuts 3 pieces which each measure 75 cm and 4 pieces which each measure 40 cm. How much wire is left on the roll?

21 Work out 453×73.

Edexcel

22 Car Hire Co. have the following cars available to rent.

Model	Number of cars	Weekly rental
Corsa	10	£210
Astra	12	£255
Zafira	6	£289

Work out the total weekly rental when all the cars are hired.

23 Lauren works in a car factory. She inspects 14 cars a day. Last year she inspected 3052 cars.
For how many days did she work last year?

24 Tom breeds hamsters for pet shops. The number of hamsters trebles each year.
Tom has 20 hamsters at the end of Year 1.
(a) How many hamsters would Tom have at the end of 5 years?
(b) A hamster cage can hold no more than 14 hamsters.
Work out the minimum number of cages needed for 900 hamsters.

Edexcel

25 Look at these calculations, they show the beginning of a number pattern.

① $1 = \frac{1 \times 2}{2} = 1$ ② $1 + 2 = \frac{2 \times 3}{2} = 3$ ③ $1 + 2 + 3 = \frac{3 \times 4}{2} = 6$

(a) Complete the next calculation in the pattern: ④ $1 + 2 + 3 + 4 = \ldots = \ldots$
(b) Hence, work out the sum of the first 100 whole number.

SECTION 2 — Decimals

What you need to know

- You should be able to write decimals in order by considering place value.

  Eg 1 Write the decimals 4.1, 4.001, 4.15, 4.01, and 4.2 in order, smallest first.
  4.001, 4.01, 4.1, 4.15, 4.2

- Be able to use non-calculator methods to add and subtract decimals.

  Eg 2 2.8 + 0.56
  $$\begin{array}{r} 2.8 \\ +\ 0.56 \\ \hline 3.36 \\ \hline {\scriptstyle 1} \end{array}$$

  Eg 3 9.5 − 0.74
  $$\begin{array}{r} {\scriptstyle 8,14,1} \\ 9.50 \\ -\ 0.74 \\ \hline 8.76 \end{array}$$

  Addition and Subtraction
  Keep the decimal points in a vertical column.
  9.5 can be written as 9.50.

- You should be able to multiply and divide decimals by powers of 10 (10, 100, 1000, …)

  Eg 4 Work out.
  (a) $6.7 \times 100 = 670$
  (b) $0.35 \times 10 = 3.5$
  (c) $5.4 \div 10 = 0.54$
  (d) $4.6 \div 100 = 0.046$

- Be able to use non-calculator methods to multiply and divide decimals by other decimals.

  Eg 5 0.43×5.1
  $$\begin{array}{r} 0.43\ \ (\text{2 d.p.}) \\ \times\ \ \ 5.1\ \ (\text{1 d.p.}) \\ \hline 43\ \ \leftarrow 43 \times 1 \\ +\ 2150\ \ \leftarrow 43 \times 50 \\ \hline 2.193\ \ (\text{3 d.p.}) \end{array}$$

  Multiplication
  Ignore the decimal points and multiply the numbers.
  Count the total number of decimal places in the question.
  The answer has the same total number of decimal places.

  Eg 6 $1.64 \div 0.2$
  $\frac{1.64}{0.2} = \frac{16.4}{2} = 8.2$

  Division
  It is easier to divide by a whole number than by a decimal.
  So, multiply the numerator and denominator by a power of 10 (10, 100, …) to make the dividing number a whole number.

- Be able to use decimal notation for money and other measures.

  The metric and common imperial units you need to know are given in Section 33.

- Be able to change decimals to fractions.

  Eg 7 (a) $0.2 = \frac{2}{10} = \frac{1}{5}$ (b) $0.65 = \frac{65}{100} = \frac{13}{20}$ (c) $0.07 = \frac{7}{100}$

- Be able to carry out a variety of calculations involving decimals.

- Know that when a number is:
  multiplied by a number between 0 and 1 the result will be **smaller** than the original number,
  divided by a number between 0 and 1 the result will be **larger** than the original number.

Exercise 2

Do not use a calculator for questions 1 to 16.

1 Look at this collection of numbers.
Two of these numbers are multiplied together.
Which two numbers will give the smallest answer?

13.5   0.065   0.9   4.5   23.0

2 Write the decimals 1.18, 1.80, 1.08, 1.118 in order, smallest first.

3 Work out.
(a) 12.08 + 6.51   (b) 6.8 + 4.57   (c) 4.7 − 1.8   (d) 5.0 − 2.36

4 Toyah buys the following vegetables.
   0.55 kg onions   1.2 kg carrots   2.5 kg potatoes   0.65 kg leeks
What is the total weight of the vegetables?

5 A tin of paint costs £8.99
Find the total cost of 3 tins of paint.   *Edexcel*

6 Henry bought 2 pencils at 28p each, 4 pads of paper at £1.20 each and 1 magazine at £2.95.
He paid with a £10 note.
How much change should Henry get from £10?   *Edexcel*

7 (a) Multiply 3.2 by 100.   (b) Divide 3.2 by 10.

8 (a) Work out 700×0.8 in your head. Explain your method.
  (b) Work out $60 \div 0.4$ in your head. Explain your method.

9 Two pieces of wood of length 0.75 m and 2.68 m are sawn from a plank 5 m long.
What length of wood is left?

10 (a) Lucy works out 0.2×0.4. She gets the answer 0.8.
   Explain why her answer must be wrong.
  (b) Work out (i) 0.3×0.4,   (ii) 0.3×0.2.

11 Work out. (a) (i) 13.4×0.3 (ii) 4.8×2.5
         (b) (i) $54.4 \div 0.4$ (ii) $0.294 \div 1.2$

12 Using the calculation $23 \times 32 = 736$,   work out the following.
  (a) 2.3×3.2 (b) $73.6 \div 23$ (c) $736 \div 3.2$

13 Tim paid £5.44 for 17 pencils. Each pencil costs the same.
Work out the cost of each pencil.   *Edexcel*

14 Write as a fraction.   (a) 0.3   (b) 0.03   (c) 0.33

15 Kevin is working out the time needed to complete a journey.

Using his calculator, he gets the answer 0.66666666
The result is in hours.
How many minutes will the journey take?

16 $5 \times m$ gives an answer **less than 5**. $5 \div m$ gives an answer **more than 5**.
Give two possible values for *m* which satisfy **both** conditions.

17 Potatoes are sold in bags and sacks.
Bags of potatoes weigh 2.5 kg and cost 95 pence.
Sacks of potatoes weigh 12 kg and cost £3.18.
How much, per kilogram, is saved by buying sacks of potatoes instead of bags of potatoes?

18 Apples cost 99p per kilogram. Work out the total cost of 3.65 kg of apples.   *Edexcel*

19 The distance by road from Maidstone to Manchester is approximately 250 miles.
Work out an estimate for this distance in kilometres, given that 1 kilometre is about 0.62 miles.
                                                                                                                                  Edexcel

20 Work out $\dfrac{12.9 \times 7.3}{3.9 + 1.4}$.   Write down your full calculator display.

SECTION

What you need to know

- How to **round** to the nearest 10, 100, 1000.

  Eg 1 Write 6473 to (a) the nearest 10, (b) the nearest 100, (c) the nearest 1000.
  (a) 6470, (b) 6500, (c) 6000.

- In real-life problems a rounding must be used which gives a sensible answer.

  Eg 2 Doughnuts are sold in packets of 6. Tessa needs 20 doughnuts for a party. How many packets of doughnuts must she buy?

  $20 \div 6 = 3.33\ldots$ This should be rounded up to 4. So, Tessa must buy 4 packets.

- How to approximate using **decimal places**.

  Write the number using one more decimal place than asked for.
  Look at the last decimal place and
  - if the figure is 5 or more round up,
  - if the figure is less than 5 round down.

  Eg 3 Write the number 3.649 to
  (a) 2 decimal places,
  (b) 1 decimal place.

  (a) 3.65,
  (b) 3.6.

- How to approximate using **significant figures**.

  Start from the most significant figure and count the required number of figures.
  Look at the next figure to the right of this and
  - if the figure is 5 or more round up,
  - if the figure is less than 5 round down.
  Add noughts, as necessary, to preserve the place value.

  Eg 4 Write each of these numbers correct to 2 significant figures.
  (a) 365
  (b) 0.0423

  (a) 370
  (b) 0.042

- You should be able to choose a suitable degree of accuracy.

  > The result of a calculation involving measurement should not be given to a greater degree of accuracy than the measurements used in the calculation.

- Be able to use approximations to estimate that the actual answer to a calculation is of the right order of magnitude.

  Eg 5 Use approximations to estimate $\frac{5.1 \times 57.2}{9.8}$.

  $\frac{5.1 \times 57.2}{9.8} = \frac{5 \times 60}{10} = 30$

  > Estimation is done by approximating every number in the calculation to one significant figure.
  > The calculation is then done using the approximated values.

- Be able to use a calculator to check answers to calculations.
- Be able to recognise limitations on the accuracy of data and measurements.

  Eg 6 Jamie said, "I have 60 friends at my party." This figure is correct to the nearest 10. What is the smallest and largest possible number of friends Jamie had at his party?

  The smallest whole number that rounds to 60 is 55.
  The largest whole number that rounds to 60 is 64.
  So, smallest is 55 friends and largest is 64 friends.

  Eg 7 A man weighs 57 kg, correct to the nearest kilogram. What is the minimum weight of the man?
  Minimum weight = 57 kg − 0.5 kg = 56.5 kg.

Exercise 3

Do not use a calculator for questions 1 to 20.

1. Write the result shown on the calculator display
   (a) to the nearest whole number,
   (b) to the nearest ten,
   (c) to the nearest hundred.

   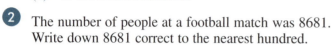

2. The number of people at a football match was 8681.
   Write down 8681 correct to the nearest hundred. *Edexcel*

3. A newspaper's headline states: "20 000 people attend concert".
   The number in the newspaper is given to the nearest thousand.
   What is the smallest possible attendance?

4. The diagram shows the distances between towns A, B and C.

   By rounding each of the distances given to the nearest hundred, estimate the distance between A and C.

5. Wayne is calculating $\dfrac{8961}{1315 + 1692}$.
   (a) Write down each of the numbers 8961, 1315 and 1692 to the nearest hundred.
   (b) Hence, estimate the value of $\dfrac{8961}{1315 + 1692}$.

6. On Saturday a dairy sold 2975 litres of milk at 42 pence per litre.
   By rounding each number to one significant figure, estimate the amount of money received from the sale of milk, giving your answer in pounds.

7. Socks cost £2.85 a pair. Afzal has £15.
   Afzal estimates in his head how many pairs of socks he could buy for £15.
   (a) Write down a sum he could do in his head.
   (b) Use your sum to estimate how many pairs of socks Afzal could buy. *Edexcel*

8. (a) Write down two numbers you could use to get an approximate answer to 41 × 89.
   (b) Work out your approximate answer.
   (c) Work out the difference between your approximate answer and the exact answer. *Edexcel*

9. (a) Show how you could find an estimate for 2019 ÷ 37.
   (b) What is your estimated answer?

10. (a) To estimate 97 × 49, Charlie uses the approximations 100 × 50.
        Explain why his estimate will be larger than the actual answer.
    (b) To estimate 1067 ÷ 48, Patsy uses the approximations 1000 ÷ 50.
        Will her estimate be larger or smaller than the actual answer?
        Give a reason for your answer.

11. A concert hall has 22 rows of seats. Each row has 69 seats.
    (a) Work out an approximate answer to the total number of seats in the concert hall.

    Every person attending a concert pays £9.75 on entry. Every seat in the concert hall is filled.
    (b) Work out the approximate amount of money taken at the concert hall. *Edexcel*

12. A car park has spaces for 640 cars, correct to the nearest ten.
    (a) What is the least possible number of spaces in the car park?
    (b) What is the greatest possible number of spaces in the car park?

13. Jenny said that the length of her book is 21.335 cm.
    The length given by Jenny is not sensible.
    Explain why her answer is not sensible. *Edexcel*

14 The length of a garden is 50 m, correct to the nearest metre.
What is the minimum length of the garden?

15 Tickets for a concert cost £9 each. Ramana has £50.
Work out the greatest number of tickets that Ramana can buy. *Edexcel*

16 Melanie needs 200 crackers for an office party.
The crackers are sold in boxes of 12.
How many boxes must she buy?

17 Clint has to calculate $\frac{414 + 198}{36}$.
He calculates the answer to be 419.5.
By rounding each number to one significant figure, estimate whether his answer is about right.
Show all your working.

18 Estimate the value of $\frac{68 \times 401}{198}$. *Edexcel*

19 (a) Write 37 451 correct to one significant figure.
(b) Write 0.000 726 9 correct to one significant figure. *Edexcel*

20 Explain how you can **estimate** the value of the following by approximating the three numbers
and give your approximate answer. $\frac{0.251 \times 81.376}{5.096}$ *Edexcel*

21 (a) Find an approximate value of $\frac{21 \times 58}{112}$.
(b) Use a calculator to find the difference between your approximate value and the exact value.

22 In 2005, Mr Symms drove 8873 kilometres.
His car does 11 kilometres per litre. Petrol costs 89.9 pence per litre.
(a) By rounding each number to one significant figure, estimate the amount he spent on petrol.
(b) Without any further calculation, explain why this estimate will be larger than the actual amount.

23 Georgina said, "I spent £100 on my holidays." This amount is given correct to the nearest £10.
Write down the minimum and maximum amounts Georgina could have spent.

24 Calculate 97.2 ÷ 6.5.
Give your answer correct to (a) two decimal places, (b) one decimal place.

25 Calculate 78.4 × 8.7.
Give your answer correct to (a) two significant figures, (b) one significant figure.

26 Andrew says, "Answers given to two decimal places are more accurate than answers given
to two significant figures." Is he right? Explain your answer.

27 Calculate the value of $\frac{65.4}{4.3 + 3.58}$.
(a) Write down your full calculator display.
(b) Give your answer correct to 3 significant figures.

28 Use your calculator to evaluate the following. $\frac{50 - 19.7}{31.6 + 55.1}$
Give your answer correct to one decimal place.

29 (a) Calculate $\frac{88.3 \times 4.24}{72.5 - 9.87}$.
(b) By using approximations show that your answer to (a) is about right.
You **must** show all your working. *Edexcel*

SECTION 4 Negative Numbers

What you need to know

- You should be able to use **negative numbers** in context, such as temperature, bank accounts.
- Realise where negative numbers come on a **number line**.

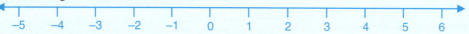

- Be able to put numbers in order (including negative numbers).

  Eg 1 Write the numbers 19, −3, 7, −5 and 0 in order, starting with the smallest.

  −5, −3, 0, 7, 19

- You should be able to add, subtract, multiply and divide with negative numbers.

  Eg 2 Work out.
  (a) −3 + 10   (b) −5 − 7   (c) −4 × 5   (d) −12 ÷ 4
      = 7   = −12   = −20   = −3

- Be able to use these rules with negative numbers.

When adding or subtracting:	When multiplying:	When dividing:
+ + can be replaced by +	+ × + = +	+ ÷ + = +
− − can be replaced by +	− × − = +	− ÷ − = +
+ − can be replaced by −	+ × − = −	+ ÷ − = −
− + can be replaced by −	− × + = −	− ÷ + = −

  Eg 3 Work out.
  (a) (−3) + (−2)   (b) (−5) − (−8)   (c) (−2) × (−3)   (d) (−8) ÷ (+2)
      = −3 − 2   = −5 + 8   = 6   = −4
      = −5   = 3

Exercise 4

Do not use a calculator for this exercise.

1 What temperatures are shown by these thermometers?

(a) 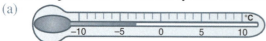 (b)

2 The midday temperatures in three different places on the same day are shown.

Moscow −7°C   Oslo −9°C   Warsaw −5°C

(a) Which place was coldest?
(b) Which place was warmest?

3 The top of a cliff is 125 m above sea level. The bottom of a lake is 15 m below sea level. How far is the bottom of the lake below the top of the cliff?

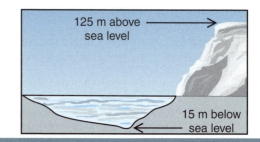

4 Place the following numbers in order of size, starting with the smallest.

17   −9   −3   5   0   7

5 Work out. (a) −5 + 10   (b) −10 − 5   (c) −5 × 10   (d) −10 ÷ 5

6 The table shows the maximum and minimum temperatures for five cities during one year.

City	Chicago	Bombay	London	Montreal	Reykjavik
Maximum	30°C	37°C	34°C	26°C	17°C
Minimum	−15°C	12°C	−12°C	−17°C	−14°C

(a) Which city had the lowest temperature?
(b) Work out the difference between the maximum temperature and the minimum temperature for Chicago.

Edexcel

7 Gordon has £28 in his bank account.
He pays a bill of £85 by cheque, which is accepted by his bank.
What is the new balance in his account?

8 The table shows the temperatures recorded at a ski resort one day in February.

Time	0600	1200	1800	2400
Temperature (°C)	−3	3	−2	−6

(a) By how many degrees did the temperature rise between 0600 and 1200?
(b) During which six-hourly period was the maximum drop in temperature recorded?

9 One evening last winter the temperature in Cardiff was 3°C, in Belfast was −4°C and in Edinburgh was −10°C.
(a) Work out the difference in temperature between
   (i) Cardiff and Belfast,   (ii) Edinburgh and Belfast.
(b) The temperature in Belfast increased by 6°C. Work out the new temperature in Belfast.
(c) The temperature in Edinburgh fell by 5°C. Work out the new temperature in Edinburgh.

Edexcel

10 Find the missing numbers so that each row adds up to 5.

(a) | | −2 | 3 | | (b) | −2 | | −4 | (c) | | 9 | −1 |

11 The ice cream is stored at −25°C.
How many degrees is this below the required storage temperature?

12 Find the value of (a) −7 − (−3),   (b) −2 × 4.

Edexcel

13 Work out. (a) (i) (+5) × (−4)   (ii) (−7) × (−3)
         (b) (i) (−12) ÷ (+3)   (ii) (−15) ÷ (−5)

14 This rule can be used to estimate the temperature in °F for temperatures given in °C.

> Multiply the temperature in °C by 2 and add 30.

Use this rule to estimate −5°C in °F.

15 Work out. (a) $\dfrac{(-2) \times (-5) \times (+6)}{(-3)}$ (b) (−3) + (−2) × (+6)

16 A test has 12 questions.

> A correct answer scores +3 marks.   An incorrect answer scores −1 mark.

Pippa attempts every question and scores 8 marks.
How many correct answers did she get?

SECTION 5 Fractions

What you need to know

- The top number of a fraction is called the **numerator**, the bottom number is called the **denominator**.

- Fractions which are equal are called **equivalent fractions**.

  To write an equivalent fraction:
  Multiply the numerator and denominator by the **same** number.

  Eg 1 $\frac{1}{4} = \frac{1 \times 3}{4 \times 3} = \frac{1 \times 5}{4 \times 5}$

  $\frac{1}{4} = \frac{3}{12} = \frac{5}{20}$

- Fractions can be **simplified** if both the numerator and denominator can be divided by the **same number**. This is sometimes called **cancelling**.

  Eg 2 Write $\frac{20}{28}$ as a fraction in its simplest form.
  $\frac{20}{28} = \frac{20 \div 4}{28 \div 4} = \frac{5}{7}$

  Divide the numerator and denominator by the largest number that divides into both.

- $2\frac{1}{2}$ is an example of a **mixed number**.
  It is a mixture of whole numbers and fractions.

- $\frac{5}{2}$ is an **improper** (or '**top heavy**') fraction.

- Fractions must have the **same denominator** before **adding** or **subtracting**.

  Eg 3 Work out.
  (a) $\frac{4}{5} - \frac{1}{2} = \frac{8}{10} - \frac{5}{10} = \frac{3}{10}$
  (b) $2\frac{3}{4} + 1\frac{2}{3} = 2\frac{9}{12} + 1\frac{8}{12} = 3\frac{17}{12} = 4\frac{5}{12}$

  Add (or subtract) the numerators only. When the answer is an improper fraction change it into a mixed number.

- You should be able to multiply and divide fractions.

  Eg 4 Work out.
  (a) $\frac{3}{4} \times \frac{2}{3} = \frac{\cancel{3}^1}{\cancel{4}_2} \times \frac{\cancel{2}^1}{\cancel{3}_1} = \frac{1}{2}$

  The working can be simplified by cancelling.

  (b) $\frac{3}{4} \div \frac{2}{3} = \frac{3}{4} \times \frac{3}{2} = \frac{9}{8} = 1\frac{1}{8}$

  Dividing by $\frac{2}{3}$ is the same as multiplying by $\frac{3}{2}$.

- All fractions can be written as decimals.

  To change a fraction to a decimal divide the **numerator** by the **denominator**.

  Eg 5 Change $\frac{4}{5}$ to a decimal.
  $\frac{4}{5} = 4 \div 5 = 0.8$

- Some decimals have **recurring digits**.
  These are shown by:

  a single dot above a single recurring digit,

  Eg 6 $\frac{2}{3} = 0.6666... = 0.\dot{6}$

  a dot above the first and last digit of a set of recurring digits.

  Eg 7 $\frac{5}{11} = 0.454545... = 0.\dot{4}\dot{5}$

Exercise 5

Do not use a calculator for this exercise.

1 (a) What fraction of this rectangle is shaded?

(b) Copy and shade $\frac{2}{3}$ of this rectangle.

2 Which of these fractions are **not** equal to $\frac{1}{4}$?

$$\frac{2}{8} \quad \frac{3}{9} \quad \frac{4}{16} \quad \frac{6}{24} \quad \frac{7}{35}$$

3 (a) Which of the fractions $\frac{7}{10}$ or $\frac{4}{5}$ is the smaller? Explain why.
(b) Write down a fraction that lies halfway between $\frac{1}{3}$ and $\frac{1}{2}$.

4 Write these fractions in order of size. Start with the smallest fraction. $\frac{7}{12}, \frac{5}{6}, \frac{2}{3}$. *Edexcel*

5 Work out $\frac{1}{5}$ of £40.

6 This rule can be used to change kilometres into miles.

Multiply the number of kilometres by $\frac{5}{8}$

Flik cycles 24 kilometres. How many miles is this?

7 Jan uses $\frac{3}{4}$ of a jar of cherries to make a cheesecake.
How many jars of cherries does she need to buy to make 10 cheesecakes?

8 Write £250 as a fraction of £600.
Give your answer as a fraction in its simplest form. *Edexcel*

9 The cake stall at a school fete has 200 fairy cakes for sale.
It sells $\frac{3}{5}$ of them at 25p each and the remainder at 20p each.
How much money does the stall get from selling fairy cakes?

10 George buys $\frac{1}{4}$ kg of jellies at £3.60 per kilogram and $\frac{1}{5}$ kg of toffees at £4.80 per kilogram.
How much change does he get from £5?

11 Amanda buys a washing machine. Its cost is £260.
Amanda pays a deposit of $\frac{2}{5}$ of its cost.
How much deposit does she pay? *Edexcel*

12 Ann wins £160. She gives $\frac{1}{4}$ of £160 to Pat, $\frac{3}{8}$ of £160 to John and £28 to Peter.
What fraction of the £160 does Ann keep? Give your fraction in its simplest form. *Edexcel*

13 Work out. (a) $\frac{1}{6} + \frac{4}{9}$ (b) $\frac{3}{7} \div 8$ *Edexcel*

14 (a) Change $\frac{1}{6}$ to a decimal. Give the answer correct to 3 d.p.
(b) Write these numbers in order of size, starting with the largest.

$$1.067 \quad 1.7 \quad 1.66 \quad 1\frac{1}{6} \quad 1.67$$

15 Work out. (a) $\frac{1}{4} \times \frac{2}{3}$ (b) $2\frac{3}{8} - 1\frac{1}{4}$ *Edexcel*

16 Asif, Barbara and Curtly share some money.
Asif receives $\frac{3}{8}$ of the money. Barbara receives $\frac{1}{3}$ of the money.
What fraction of the money does Curtly receive? *Edexcel*

17 Work out $\frac{2}{3} \times \frac{5}{6}$. Give your answer as a fraction in its simplest form. *Edexcel*

18 Three-fifths of the people at a party are boys.
Three-quarters of the boys are wearing fancy dress.
What fraction of the people at the party are boys wearing fancy dress?

19 Stuart pays £3.50 for $\frac{1}{4}$ kg of Stilton Cheese and $\frac{1}{2}$ kg of Cheddar Cheese.
Stilton Cheese costs £6.40 per kilogram. How much per kilogram is Cheddar Cheese?

SECTION  Working with Number

What you need to know

- **Multiples** of a number are found by multiplying the number by 1, 2, 3, 4, ...

  Eg 1 The multiples of 8 are $1 \times 8 = 8$, $2 \times 8 = 16$, $3 \times 8 = 24$, $4 \times 8 = 32$, ...

- **Factors** of a number are found by listing all the products that give the number.

  Eg 2 $1 \times 6 = 6$ and $2 \times 3 = 6$.
  So, the factors of 6 are: 1, 2, 3 and 6.

- The **common factors** of two numbers are the numbers which are factors of **both**.

  Eg 3 Factors of 16 are: 1, 2, 4, 8, 16.
  Factors of 24 are: 1, 2, 3, 4, 6, 8, 12, 24.
  Common factors of 16 and 24 are: 1, 2, 4, 8.

- A **prime number** is a number with only two factors, 1 and the number itself.
  The first few prime numbers are: 2, 3, 5, 7, 11, 13, 17, 19, ...
  The number 1 is not a prime number because it has only one factor.

- The **prime factors** of a number are those factors of the number which are prime numbers.

  Eg 4 The factors of 18 are: 1, 2, 3, 6, 9 and 18.
  The prime factors of 18 are: 2 and 3.

- The **Least Common Multiple** of two numbers is the smallest number that is a multiple of both.

  Eg 5 The Least Common Multiple of 4 and 5 is 20.

- The **Highest Common Factor** of two numbers is the largest number that is a factor of both.

  Eg 6 The Highest Common Factor of 8 and 12 is 4.

- An expression such as $3 \times 3 \times 3 \times 3 \times 3$ can be written in a shorthand way as 3^5.
  This is read as '3 to the power of 5'.
  The number 3 is the **base** of the expression. 5 is the **power**.

- Powers can be used to help write any number as the **product of its prime factors**.

  Eg 7 $72 = 2 \times 2 \times 2 \times 3 \times 3 = 2^3 \times 3^2$

- Numbers raised to the power of 2 are **squared**.
  For example, $3^2 = 3 \times 3 = 9$.
  Squares can be calculated using the $\boxed{x^2}$ button on a calculator.

  > **Square numbers** are whole numbers squared.
  > The first few square numbers are: 1, 4, 9, 16, 25, 36, ...

  The opposite of squaring a number is called finding the **square root**.
  Square roots can be found by using the $\boxed{\sqrt{}}$ button on a calculator.
  The square root of a number can be positive or negative.

  Eg 8 The square root of 9 is $+3$ or -3.

- You should be able to find square roots using a method called **trial and improvement**.
  Work methodically using trials first to the nearest whole number, then to one decimal place, etc.
  Do one trial to one more decimal place than the required accuracy to be sure of your answer.

- Numbers raised to the power of 3 are **cubed**.
  For example, $4^3 = 4 \times 4 \times 4 = 64$.

  > **Cube numbers** are whole numbers cubed.
  > The first few cube numbers are: 1, 8, 27, 64, 125, ...

  The opposite of cubing a number is called finding the **cube root**.

  Cube roots can be found by using the $\boxed{\sqrt[3]{\ }}$ button on a calculator.

- **Powers**

  The squares and cubes of numbers can be worked out on a calculator by using the $\boxed{x^y}$ button.

  The $\boxed{x^y}$ button can be used to calculate the value of a number x raised to the power of y.

  Eg 9 Calculate 2.6^4.
  Enter the sequence: $\boxed{2}\ \boxed{.}\ \boxed{6}\ \boxed{x^y}\ \boxed{4}\ \boxed{=}$. So, $2.6^4 = 45.6976$.

- The **reciprocal** of a number is the value obtained when the number is divided into 1.

  Eg 10 The reciprocal of 2 is $\frac{1}{2}$.

  The reciprocal of a number can be found on a calculator by using the $\boxed{\frac{1}{x}}$ button.
  A number times its reciprocal equals 1. Zero has no reciprocal.

- You should be able to simplify calculations involving powers.
  Powers of the same base are **added** when terms are **multiplied**.
  Powers of the same base are **subtracted** when terms are **divided**.

  > In general:
  > $a^m \times a^n = a^{m+n}$
  > $a^m \div a^n = a^{m-n}$

  Eg 11 (a) $2^3 \times 2^2 = 2^5$ (b) $2^3 \div 2^2 = 2^1 = 2$

You should be able to:

- use the $\boxed{x^2}$, $\boxed{x^y}$, $\boxed{\sqrt{\ }}$ and $\boxed{\frac{1}{x}}$ buttons on a calculator to solve a variety of problems.

- interpret a calculator display for very large and very small numbers expressed in standard index form.

  Eg 12 $\boxed{1.5 \qquad 10}$ means $1.5 \times 10^{10} = 15\,000\,000\,000$

  $\boxed{6.2 \qquad -05}$ means $6.2 \times 10^{-5} = 0.000\,062$

Exercise 6

Do not use a calculator for questions 1 to 19.

1. From the numbers in the cloud, write down
   (a) those numbers that 2 will divide into exactly,
   (b) those numbers that 10 will divide into exactly,
   (c) the number which is double one of the other numbers.

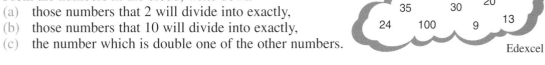

   25, 27, 12, 35, 30, 20, 24, 100, 9, 13

   Edexcel

2. (a) Write down all the factors of 18.
   (b) Write down a multiple of 7 between 30 and 40.
   (c) Explain why 9 is not a prime number.

3. 2   8   15   17   25   35
   Write down a number from this list that is   (a) a square number,   (b) a cube number.

   Edexcel

4. (a) What is the square of 6?
   (b) What is the square root of 100?

5. Jenny says that $2^2 + 3^2 = (2 + 3)^2$. Is she right? Show your working.

6. Here is a list of numbers. 8   15   23   27   32   33
   From the numbers in the list, write down a number that is prime.

   Edexcel

7 Find the common factors of 18 and 24.

8 Write down the value of (a) $\sqrt{25}$, (b) the cube of 4. *Edexcel*

9 Find the value of (a) $1^2 + 2^2 + 3^2 + 4^2 + 5^2$, (b) $9^2 \times 10^2$, (c) $2^3 \times 5^2$.

10 Richard says that $1^3 + 2^3 = 3^3$. Is he right? Show your working.

11 Work out. (a) $2^3 \times 3^2$ (b) $\sqrt{25} + \sqrt{144}$ (c) $\sqrt{49} \times 4^2$

12 Find the value of $\sqrt{(2 \times 2 \times 3 \times 3 \times 5 \times 5)}$ *Edexcel*

13 (a) Write 36 as a product of its prime factors.
(b) Write 45 as a product of its prime factors.
(c) What is the highest common factor of 36 and 45?
(d) What is the least common multiple of 36 and 45?

14 Find the highest common factor of 108 and 180. *Edexcel*

15 A white light flashes every 10 seconds. A red light flashes every 6 seconds.
The two lights flash at the same time.
After how many seconds will the lights next flash at the same time?

16 (a) What is the cube root of 125?
(b) What is the reciprocal of 4?
(c) Which is smaller $\sqrt{225}$ or 2^4? Show your working.

17 Find the value of x in each of the following. (a) $7^6 \times 7^3 = 7^x$ (b) $7^6 \div 7^3 = 7^x$

18 Simplify fully each of these expressions. Leave your answers in power form.
(a) $3^2 \times 3^3$ (b) $5^6 \div 5^3$ (c) $\dfrac{2 \times 2^3}{2^2}$

19 (a) Work out 2.5×10^6.
(b) Write down the number on this calculator display. $\boxed{3.7 \quad -0.5}$

20 Find the value of the square root of 1.5625. *Edexcel*

21 (a) Between which two consecutive whole numbers does $\sqrt{70}$ lie?
(b) Use a trial and improvement method to find the square root of 70 correct to two decimal places. Show your working clearly.

22 (a) Find the reciprocal of 7, correct to two decimal places.
(b) Find the value of 5.6^3.

23 Use a calculator to work out $15.2 \times \sqrt{10.24} - 3.62$. *Edexcel*

24 (a) Use your calculator to find the value of $5.43 \times \sqrt{(18 - 6.67)}$.
Write down all the figures on your calculator display.
(b) Give your answer to part (a) correct to 2 decimal places. *Edexcel*

25 Use your calculator to find the value of $\sqrt{(4.73^2 - 9.1^2)}$.
(a) Write down all the figures on your calculator display.
(b) Write your answer to part (a) correct to 2 significant figures. *Edexcel*

26 Use your calculator to work out the value of $\dfrac{\sqrt{12.3^2 + 7.9}}{1.8 \times 0.17}$.
Give your answer correct to 1 decimal place. *Edexcel*

27 (a) Calculate the value of $\sqrt{\dfrac{4.1}{(0.19)^2}}$.
(b) Show how to check that your answer is of the right order of magnitude.

SECTION 7 Percentages

What you need to know

- 10% is read as '10 percent'. 'Per cent' means out of 100. 10% means 10 out of 100.
- A percentage can be written as a fraction, 10% can be written as $\frac{10}{100}$.
- To change a decimal or a fraction to a percentage: **multiply by 100**.

  Eg 1 Write as a percentage (a) 0.12 (b) $\frac{8}{25}$

  (a) $0.12 \times 100 = 12\%$ (b) $\frac{8}{25} \times 100 = 32\%$

- To change a percentage to a fraction or a decimal: **divide by 100**.

  Eg 2 Write 18% as (a) a decimal, (b) a fraction.

  (a) $18\% = 18 \div 100 = 0.18$, (b) $18\% = \frac{18}{100} = \frac{9}{50}$.

- How to express one quantity as a percentage of another.

  Eg 3 Write 30p as a percentage of £2.
  $\frac{30}{200} \times 100 = 30 \times 100 \div 200 = 15\%$

  > Write the numbers as a fraction, using the same units.
  > Change the fraction to a percentage.

- You should be able to use percentages to solve a variety of problems.
- Be able to find a percentage of a quantity.

  Eg 4 Find 20% of £64.
  £64 ÷ 100 = £0.64
  £0.64 × 20 = £12.80

  > 1. Divide by 100 to find 1%.
  > 2. Multiply by the percentage to be found.

- Be able to find a percentage increase (or decrease).

  > Percentage increase = $\frac{\text{actual increase}}{\text{initial value}} \times 100\%$
  >
  > Percentage decrease = $\frac{\text{actual decrease}}{\text{initial value}} \times 100\%$

  Eg 5 Find the percentage loss on a micro-scooter bought for £25 and sold for £18.
  Percentage loss = $\frac{7}{25} \times 100 = 28\%$

Exercise 7

Do not use a calculator for questions 1 to 14.

1 What percentage of these rectangles are shaded?

(a) 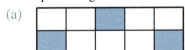 (b) (c)

2 Write $\frac{1}{2}$, 0.02 and 20% in order of size, smallest first.

3 Work out (a) 10% of 20 pence, (b) 25% of 60 kg, (c) 5% of £900.

4 In an examination, Felicity scored 75% of the marks and Daisy scored $\frac{4}{5}$ of the marks. Who has the better score? Give a reason for your answer.

5 Work out 30% of £45.

6 In a survey, 500 people were questioned about things they recycled.
25% of the people said they recycled paper.
How many people is this?

7 A pop concert is attended by 35 000 people.
2% of the people are given a free T-shirt.
How many people are given a free T-shirt?

8 Andy is given £4 pocket money. He spends 15% of it on a magazine.
How much was the magazine?

9 Work out 45% of 800.

10 Mira earns £600 a week. She is given a pay rise of £30 a week.
What is the percentage increase in her pay?

11 Class 11A has 30 pupils. 18 of these pupils are girls.
What percentage of the class is girls?

12 180 college students apply for jobs at a new supermarket.
 (a) 70% of the students are given an interview.
  How many students are given an interview?
 (b) 54 students are offered jobs.
  What percentage of the students who applied were offered jobs?

13 A mobile phone normally costs £90. The price is reduced by 20% in a sale.
What is the price of the mobile phone in the sale?

14 Maggie normally works Monday to Friday and is paid £6.50 per hour.
When she works on a Saturday she is paid 30% **more**.
How much is she paid per hour for working on a Saturday?

15 Lisa had £10.50. She gave 8% to charity and kept the rest of the money.
Work out how much money she kept.

16 In an experiment a spring is extended from 12 cm to 15 cm.
Calculate the percentage increase in the length of the spring.

17 Find the percentage reduction on the
Mega Ace Games System in the sale.

MEGA ACE GAMES SYSTEM
Normal Price £320
Sale Price £272

18 You have to climb 123 steps to see the view from the top of a tower.
Harold has climbed 66 steps.
What percentage of the steps has he still got to climb?
Give your answer to the nearest whole number.

19 A farmer has 200 sheep.
90% of the sheep have lambs.
Of the sheep which have lambs 45% have two lambs.
How many of the sheep have two lambs?

20 A shop buys Indian rugs from a factory.
In July, the cost to the shop of buying a rug was £100.
The shop bought 800 rugs in July.
In August, the cost to the shop of buying a rug increased by 10%.
The number of rugs bought by the shop decreased by 25%.
Find the difference between the total cost to the shop of all the rugs bought in July and the total cost of all the rugs bought by the shop in August.

SECTION 8 — Time and Money

What you need to know

- Time can be given using either the **12-hour clock** or the **24-hour clock**.

  Eg 1 (a) 1120 is equivalent to 11.20 am.
  (b) 1645 is equivalent to 4.45 pm.

  When using the 12-hour clock: times **before** midday are given as am, times **after** midday are given as pm.

- **Timetables** are usually given using the 24-hour clock.

  Eg 2 Some of the rail services from Manchester to Stoke are shown.

Manchester	0925	1115	1215	1415	1555
Stockport	0933	—	1223	—	1603
Stoke	1007	1155	1255	1459	1636

  Some trains do not stop at every station. This is shown by a dash on the timetable.

  Kath catches the 1555 from Manchester to Stoke.
  (a) How many minutes does the journey take?
  (b) What is her arrival time in 12-hour clock time?

  (a) 41 minutes.
  (b) 4.36 pm.

- When considering a **best buy**, compare quantities by using the same units.

  Eg 3 Peanut butter is available in small or large jars.
  Small jar: 250 grams for 68 pence.   Large jar: 454 grams for £1.25.
  Which size is the better value for money?

  Small jar: $250 \div 68 = 3.67\ldots$ grams per penny.
  Large jar: $454 \div 125 = 3.63\ldots$ grams per penny.
  The small jar gives more grams per penny and is better value.

  Compare the number of grams per penny for each size.

- **Value added tax**, or **VAT**, is a tax on some goods and services and is added to the bill.

  Eg 4 A freezer costs £180 + $17\tfrac{1}{2}$% VAT.

  $17\tfrac{1}{2}\% = 17.5\% = \tfrac{17.5}{100} = 0.175$

  (a) How much is the VAT?
  (b) What is the total cost of the freezer?

  (a) VAT = £180 × 0.175 = £31.50
  (b) Total cost = £180 + £31.50 = £211.50

- **Exchange rates** are used to show what £1 will buy in foreign currencies.

  Eg 5 Alex buys a painting for 80 euros in France.
  The exchange rate is 1.55 euros to the £.
  What is the cost of the painting in £s?

  1.55 euros = £1   80 euros = 80 ÷ 1.55 = £51.6129…
  The painting cost £51.61, to the nearest penny.

Exercise 8

Do not use a calculator for questions 1 to 4.

1 Tom buys the following items from a shop.

> 6 tins of baked beans at 28p each,
> 5 tins of cat food at 57p each,
> 2 packets of tea bags at £1.41 each.

(a) Work out the total cost of these items.

Tom went into the shop at 0953. He came out of the shop at 1002.
(b) For how many minutes was Tom in the shop?

Edexcel

2 Here is part of a bus timetable.

Wigan, bus station	0530	0555	0620	—	0640
Hindley Green	0552	0617	0642	—	0702
Atherton	0558	0623	0648	0700	0710
Tyldesley	0604	0629	0654	0706	0716
Monton Green	0625	0650	0715	0729	0739
Eccles	0631	0656	0722	0736	0746
Trafford Road	0636	0701	0730	0744	0754

(a) At what time should the 0620 from Wigan arrive at Monton Green?
(b) How long should it take the 0629 bus from Tyldesley to travel to Trafford Road?

Susan catches a bus in Atherton. She needs to be in Eccles by 0700.
(c) What is the time of the latest bus she could catch from Atherton?

Edexcel

3 Reg travels to Ireland. The exchange rate is 1.60 euros to the £.
(a) He changes £40 into euros. How many euros does he receive?
(b) A taxi fare costs 10 euros. What is the cost of the taxi fare in pounds and pence?

4 The table below shows the cost of hiring a wallpaper stripper.

Cost for the first day	Extra cost per day for each additional day
£7.50	£2.50

Vivian hires the wallpaper stripper. The total cost of hiring the wallpaper stripper was £35.
How many days did Vivian hire it for?

5 Wayne bought an engagement ring for Tracey.
The total cost of the ring was £420 **plus** VAT at $17\frac{1}{2}$%.
Work out the total cost of the ring.

Edexcel

6 Toffee is sold in bars of two sizes.
A large bar weighs 450 g and costs £1.69. A small bar weighs 275 g and costs 99p.
Which size of bar is better value for money? You must show all your working.

7 Prendeep bought a necklace in the United States of America.
Prendeep paid 108 dollars ($).
Arthur bought an identical necklace in Germany.
Arthur paid 117 euros (€).
Calculate, in pounds, the difference between the prices paid for the two necklaces.

£1 = $1.44
£1 = 1.6€

Edexcel

8 Mrs Tilsed wishes to buy a car priced at £2400.

Two options are available.
Option 1 –
A deposit of 20% of £2400 and 24 monthly payments of £95.
Option 2 –
For a single payment the dealer offers a discount of 5% on £2400.

How much more does it cost to buy the car if option 1 is chosen rather than option 2?

9 Sam wants to buy a Hooper washing machine.
Hooper washing machines are sold in three different shops.

Washing Power	Whytes	Clean Up
$\frac{1}{4}$ OFF usual price of £330	20% OFF usual price of £320	£210 plus VAT at 17½%

Work out the cost of the washing machine in each shop.

Edexcel

SECTION 9 **Personal Finance**

- **Hourly pay** is paid at a **basic rate** for a fixed number of hours.
  Overtime pay is usually paid at a higher rate such as time and a half, which means each hour's work is worth 1.5 times the basic rate.

  Eg 1 Alexis is paid £7.20 per hour for a basic 35-hour week.
  Overtime is paid at time and a half.
  Last week she worked 38 hours. How much was Alexis paid last week?

  Basic pay   = £7.20 × 35   = £252
  Overtime pay = 1.5 × £7.20 × 3 = £ 32.40

  Total pay   = £252 + £32.40   = £284.40

- Everyone is allowed to earn some money which is not taxed. This is called a **tax allowance**.

- Tax is only paid on income earned in excess of the tax allowance. This is called **taxable income**.

  Eg 2 Tom earns £6080 per year. His tax allowance is £4895 per year and he pays tax at 10p in the £ on his taxable income. Find how much income tax Tom pays per year.

  Taxable income   = £6080 − £4895 = £1185
  Income tax payable = £1185 × 0.10   = £118.50

  > First find the taxable income, then multiply taxable income by rate in £.

- Gas, electricity and telephone bills are paid **quarterly**.
  Some bills consist of a standing charge plus a charge for the amount used.

- Money invested in a savings account at a bank or building society earns **interest**.
  Simple Interest is when the interest is paid out each year and not added to your account.
  Simple Interest = Amount invested × Time in years × Rate of interest per year.

  Eg 3 Find the Simple Interest paid on £600 invested at 5% for 6 months.

  Simple Interest = $\frac{600}{1} \times \frac{6}{12} \times \frac{5}{100}$ = £15

  > 6 months = $\frac{6}{12}$ years.

- You should be able to work out a variety of problems involving personal finance.

Exercise 9

Do not use a calculator for questions 1 to 6.

1. Jenny worked $2\frac{1}{2}$ hours at £6.50 per hour. How much did she earn?

2. Amrit pays his council tax by 10 instalments.
   His first instalment is £193.25 and the other 9 instalments are £187 each.
   How much is his total council tax?

3. Sue insures her house for £180 000 and its contents for £14 000.
   The annual premiums for insurance are:
   House: 24p per annum for every £100 of cover.
   Contents: £1.30 per annum for every £100 of cover.
   What is the total cost of Sue's insurance?

4. Last year Harry paid the following gas bills.

   | £196.40 | £62.87 | £46.55 | £183.06 |

   This year he will pay his gas bills by 12 equal monthly payments.
   Use last year's gas bills to calculate his monthly payments.

19

5 This rule is used to work out take home pay.

$$\text{Take Home Pay} = \text{Hours Worked} \times \text{Hourly Rate} - \text{Deductions}$$

Mary's hourly rate was £6. Her deductions were £7. Her take home pay was £95.
Work out the number of hours she worked.

Edexcel

6 Travis is paid £8.67 per hour. Last week he worked 32 hours.
By using suitable approximations estimate how much he was paid for last week.
You must show all your working.

7 Esther has an annual income of £6789. She has a tax allowance of £4895.
   (a) Calculate her taxable income.

She pays tax at the rate of 10p in the £ on her taxable income.
   (b) How much income tax does she pay per year?

8 Felix is paid at time and a half for overtime. His overtime rate of pay is £8.40 per hour.
What is his basic rate of pay?

9 Here are two readings from a gas meter.

| 0 | 1 | 9 | 6 | 2 | | 0 | 2 | 1 | 5 | 9 |

January   April

The difference in the meter readings gives the number of units of gas used.
The cost of gas is 32p for each unit of gas used.
Work out the cost of gas used.

Edexcel

10 The table below shows the monthly payments for an insurance scheme.
The payments depend on the age at which a person starts paying.
There are two rates, Standard Rate and Discount Rate.

	Age	0 - 16	17 - 19	20 - 39	40 - 59	60 - 74	75 and over
Monthly Payments per Person	Standard Rate	£7.20	£12.60	£17.00	£23.40	£41.40	£84.80
	Discount Rate	£6.12	£10.71	£14.45	£19.89	£35.19	£72.08

Alison is aged 17. She pays the Standard Rate.
   (a) (i) Write down Alison's monthly payment.
       (ii) Work out the total amount Alison will pay in a year.

Mr Masih pays the Discount Rate. He pays £19.89 each month.
If he were one year older, he would have to pay £35.19 each month.
   (b) How old is Mr Masih?

Edexcel

11 Penny is paid at a basic rate of £6.84 per hour for 35 hours a week.
Overtime is paid at one and a half times the basic rate. One week Penny works 38 hours.
How much is Penny paid that week?

12 A monthly income bond pays 6% simple interest per year.
Interest is paid monthly. John invests £15 000.
How much interest is he paid each month?

13 Leroy earns £13 880 per year.
He has a tax allowance of £4895 and pays tax at the rate of 10p in the £ on the first £2090
of his taxable income and 22p in the £ on the remainder.
How much income tax does he pay each year?

14 Mr Holland uses 367 units of electricity in one month.
He pays 7.84p for each unit of electricity.
Mr Holland also pays a fixed charge of £6.14 for the month.
Work out the **total amount** he pays.

Edexcel

SECTION 10 — Ratio and Proportion

What you need to know

- The ratio 3 : 2 is read '3 to 2'.

- A ratio is used only to **compare** quantities.
  A ratio does not give information about the exact values of quantities being compared.

- Different forms of the **same ratio**, such as 2 : 1 and 6 : 3, are called **equivalent ratios**.

- In its **simplest form**, a ratio contains whole numbers which have no common factor other than 1.

  Eg 1 Write £2.40 : 40p in its simplest form.
  £2.40 : 40p = 240p : 40p
  = 240 : 40
  = 6 : 1

  All quantities in a ratio must be in the **same units** before the ratio can be simplified.

- You should be able to solve a variety of problems involving ratio.

  Eg 2 The ratio of bats to balls in a box is 2 : 3.
  There are 12 bats in the box.
  How many balls are there?

  12 ÷ 2 = 6
  2 × 6 : 3 × 6 = 12 : 18
  There are 18 balls in the box.

  For every 2 bats there are 3 balls.
  To find an equivalent ratio to 2 : 3, in which the first number is 12, multiply each number in the ratio by 6.

  Eg 3 A wall costs £600 to build.
  The costs of materials to labour are in the ratio 1 : 4.
  What is the cost of labour?

  1 + 4 = 5
  £600 ÷ 5 = £120
  Cost of labour = £120 × 4 = £480

  The numbers in the ratio add to 5.
  For every £5 of the total cost, £1 pays for materials and £4 pays for labour.
  So, **divide** by 5 and then **multiply** by 4.

- When two different quantities are always in the **same ratio** the two quantities are in **direct proportion**.

  Eg 4 20 litres of petrol cost £14.
  Find the cost of 25 litres of petrol.

  20 litres cost £14
  1 litre costs £14 ÷ 20 = £0.70
  25 litres cost £0.70 × 25 = £17.50

  This is sometimes called the **unitary method**.
  Divide by 20 to find the cost of 1 litre.
  Multiply by 25 to find the cost of 25 litres.

Exercise 10

Do not use a calculator for questions 1 to 5.

1 Write these ratios in their simplest form.
   (a) 2 : 6   (b) 8 : 4   (c) 6 : 9

2 Rhys draws a plan of his classroom floor. The classroom measures 15 m by 20 m.
He draws the plan to a scale of 1 cm to 5 m.
What are the measurements of the classroom floor on the plan?

3 A toy box contains large bricks and small bricks in the ratio 1 : 4.
The box contains 40 bricks. How many large bricks are in the box?

4 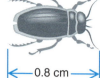 This magnifying glass makes things look bigger.
It enlarges in the ratio 1 : 5.
What is the length of the beetle under the magnifying glass?

Not to scale   0.8 cm

5 Robert used these ingredients to make 24 buns.

> 100 g of butter,   80 g of sugar,   90 g of flour,
> 2 eggs,   30 ml of milk

Robert wants to make 36 similar buns.
Write down how much of each ingredient he needs for 36 buns.

Edexcel

6 The ratio of men to women playing golf one day is 7 : 3.
(a) What percentage of the people playing golf are men?
(b) There are 21 men playing.
How many women are playing?

7 Rashid has 35 sweets.
He shares them in the ratio 4 : 3 with his sister.
Rashid keeps the larger share.
How many sweets does Rashid keep?

Edexcel

8 Dec shares a prize of £435 with Annabel in the ratio 3 : 2.
What is the difference in the amount of money they each receive?

9 To make 20 m³ of concrete for a building, the builders use:

4 m³ of cement, 12 m³ of sand and 4 m³ of ballast.

(a) What is the ratio of cement to sand?
Give your answer in its lowest terms.
(b) How much cement would be needed for 100 m³ of concrete?

Edexcel

10 Two students are talking about their school outing.

> My class went to Tower Bridge last week.
> There are 30 people in my class.
> The total cost was £345.

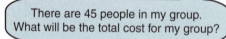

> There are 45 people in my group.
> What will be the total cost for my group?

11  Three 1-litre tins of paint cost a total of £26.85.
Find the cost of five of the 1-litre tins of paint.

Edexcel

12 On a map the distance between two towns is 5 cm.
The actual distance between the towns is 1 kilometre.
What is the scale of the map in the form of 1 : *n*?

13 Malika's father won £128.
He shared the £128 between his three children in the ratio 6 : 3 : 1.
(a) Malika was given the biggest share.
Work out how much money Malika received.
(b) Malika saved $\frac{2}{3}$ of her share.
Work out how much Malika saved.

Edexcel

SECTION 11

Speed and Other Compound Measures

What you need to know

- **Speed** is a compound measure because it involves **two** other measures.
- **Speed** is a measurement of how fast something is travelling.
  It involves two other measures, **distance** and **time**.
  In situations where speed is not constant, **average speed** is used.

  $$\text{Speed} = \frac{\text{Distance}}{\text{Time}} \qquad \text{Average speed} = \frac{\text{Total distance travelled}}{\text{Total time taken}}$$

  The formula linking speed, distance and time can be rearranged and remembered as:
  $S = D \div T$
  $D = S \times T$
  $T = D \div S$

- You should be able to solve problems involving speed, distance and time.

  Eg 1 Wyn takes 3 hours to run 24 km. Calculate his speed in kilometres per hour.

  $$\text{Speed} = \frac{\text{Distance}}{\text{Time}} = \frac{24}{3} = 8 \text{ km/h}$$

  Eg 2 Norrie says, "If I drive at an average speed of 60 km/h it will take me $2\frac{1}{2}$ hours to complete my journey."
  What distance is his journey?

  Distance = Speed × Time = $60 \times 2\frac{1}{2}$ = 150 km

  Eg 3 Ellen cycles 5 km at an average speed of 12 km/h.
  How many minutes does she take?

  $$\text{Time} = \frac{\text{Distance}}{\text{Speed}} = \frac{5}{12} \text{ hours} = \frac{5}{12} \times 60 = 25 \text{ minutes}$$

  To change hours to minutes: **multiply by 60**

- **Density** is a compound measure which involves the measures **mass** and **volume**.

  Eg 4 A block of metal has mass 500 g and volume 400 cm³.

  $$\text{Density} = \frac{\text{Mass}}{\text{Volume}} = \frac{500}{400} = 1.25 \text{ g/cm}^3$$

  $$\text{Density} = \frac{\text{Mass}}{\text{Volume}}$$

- **Population density** is a measure of how populated an area is.

  Eg 5 The population of Cumbria is 489 700.
  The area of Cumbria is 6824 km².

  $$\text{Population density} = \frac{\text{Population}}{\text{Area}}$$

  $$\text{Population density} = \frac{\text{Population}}{\text{Area}} = \frac{489\,700}{6824} = 71.8 \text{ people/km}^2.$$

Exercise 11

Do not use a calculator for questions 1 to 5.

1. Norma travels 128 km in 2 hours.
   Calculate her average speed in kilometres per hour.

2. Sean cycled 24 km at an average speed of 16 km/h.
   How long did he take to complete the journey?

3. Ahmed takes $2\frac{1}{2}$ hours to drive from New Milton to London. He averages 66 km/h.
   What distance does he drive?

4. Nigel runs 4 km at an average speed of 6 km/h.
   How many minutes does he take?

5 A lorry travels 24 miles in 30 minutes.
Calculate the average speed of the lorry in miles per hour.

6 Gail leaves home at 0950 to walk to the park.
She walks at an average speed of 5 km/h and reaches the park at 1020.
How far is the park from her home?

7 Paul takes 15 minutes to run to school. His average running speed is 8 km/h.
How far did he have to run?

8 Kay walks 2.5 km in 50 minutes.
Calculate her average walking speed in kilometres per hour.

9 Mia drove a distance of 343 km.
She took 3 hours 30 minutes.
Work our her average speed. Give your answer in km/h.

Edexcel

10 The diagram shows the distances, in miles, between some junctions on a motorway.

A coach is travelling west.
At 1040 it passes junction 27 and at 1052 it passes junction 26.
(a) Calculate the average speed of the coach in miles per hour.

Between junctions 26 and 25 the coach travels at an average speed of 30 miles per hour.
(b) Calculate the time when the coach passes junction 25.

11 The distance from London to Newcastle is 285 miles.
Paul takes $4\frac{1}{2}$ hours to drive this distance.
Calculate his average speed.

12 A train travels from Bournemouth to Manchester at an average speed of 47 miles per hour.
The train travels a distance of 268 miles.
How long does the journey take in hours and minutes?

13 A train travels at an average speed of 80 miles per hour.
At 0940 the train is 65 miles from Glasgow.
The train is due to arrive in Glasgow at 1030.
Will it arrive on time? Show your working.

14 On Monday it took Helen 40 minutes to drive to work.
On Tuesday it took Helen 25 minutes to drive to work.
Her average speed on Monday was 18 miles per hour.
What was her average speed on Tuesday?

15 In the College Games, Michael Jackson won the 200 metres race in a time of 20.32 seconds.
Calculate his average speed in metres per second.
Give your answer correct to 1 decimal place.

Edexcel

16 A jet-ski travels 0.9 kilometres in 1.5 minutes.
Calculate the average speed of the jet-ski in metres per second.

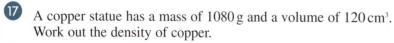

17 A copper statue has a mass of 1080 g and a volume of 120 cm³.
Work out the density of copper.

18 A silver medal has a mass of 200 g. The density of silver is 10.5 g/cm³.
What is the volume of the medal?

19 The population of Jamaica is 2.8 million people. The area of Jamaica is 10 800 km².
What is the population density of Jamaica?

Number
Non-calculator Paper

Do not use a calculator for this exercise.

1 (a) Write the number forty-five thousand six hundred and eight in figures.
(b) Write your answer to part (a) to the nearest thousand.
Edexcel

2 (a) (i) Write these numbers in order of size, smallest first: 16   10   6   100   61
(ii) What is the total when the numbers are added together?
(b) Work out. (i) $100 - 37$ (ii) 100×20 (iii) $100 \div 4$

3 $\frac{3}{4}$ of this shape is shaded.
(a) What percentage of the shape is shaded?
(b) What percentage of the shape is **not** shaded?

Edexcel

4 Orange juice is sold in cartons of two different sizes.
(a) How much is saved by buying a 500 ml carton instead of two 250 ml cartons?
(b) Reg buys four 500 ml cartons.
He pays with a £5 note.
How much change is he given?

5 The distance from London to Edinburgh via Newcastle is 600 km.
Newcastle is 176 km from Edinburgh.
How far is it from London to Newcastle?

6 An overnight train leaves Dundee at 2348 and arrives in London at 0735 the next day.
How long does the journey take? Give your answer in hours and minutes.

7 (a) Work out $40 \times 50 \times 500$.   Give your answer in words.
(b) What is the value of the 3 in the number 2439?

8 Use the numbers in the cloud to answer these questions.
(a) Which numbers are even numbers?
(b) Which numbers are multiples of 3?
(c) Which numbers are the square roots of another number in the cloud?

Edexcel

9 (a) 4 litres of milk costs £2.96. How much is 1 litre of milk?
(b) Apples cost 98 pence per kilogram. What is the cost of 5 kilograms of apples?

10 To buy a car, Ricky has to pay 24 monthly payments of £198.
How much does he have to pay altogether to buy the car?

11 Write these numbers in order of size.
Start with the largest number.

0.8   70% $\frac{7}{8}$ $\frac{3}{4}$

Edexcel

12 A ski-run measures 7.5 cm on a map. The map is drawn to a scale of 1 cm to 200 m.
What is the actual length of the ski-run in metres?

13 247 pupils and 13 teachers are going on a school visit by coach.
Each coach holds 55 passengers.
(a) How many coaches are needed?

Each coach costs £257.50 to hire.
(b) How much will the coaches cost altogether?
Edexcel

14 (a) Which of the numbers 4, 5, 6, 12 and 15 is a prime number?
(b) What are the common factors of 12 and 15?

15 Calculate. (a) 256×37 (b) $925 \div 37$
Edexcel

16 How much will it cost to hire a trailer for 5 days?

17 Write these numbers in order of size.
Start with the smallest number.
(a) 0.56, 0.067, 0.6, 0.65, 0.605.
(b) 5, −6, −10, 2, −4.
(c) $\frac{1}{2}, \frac{2}{3}, \frac{2}{5}, \frac{3}{4}$.
Edexcel

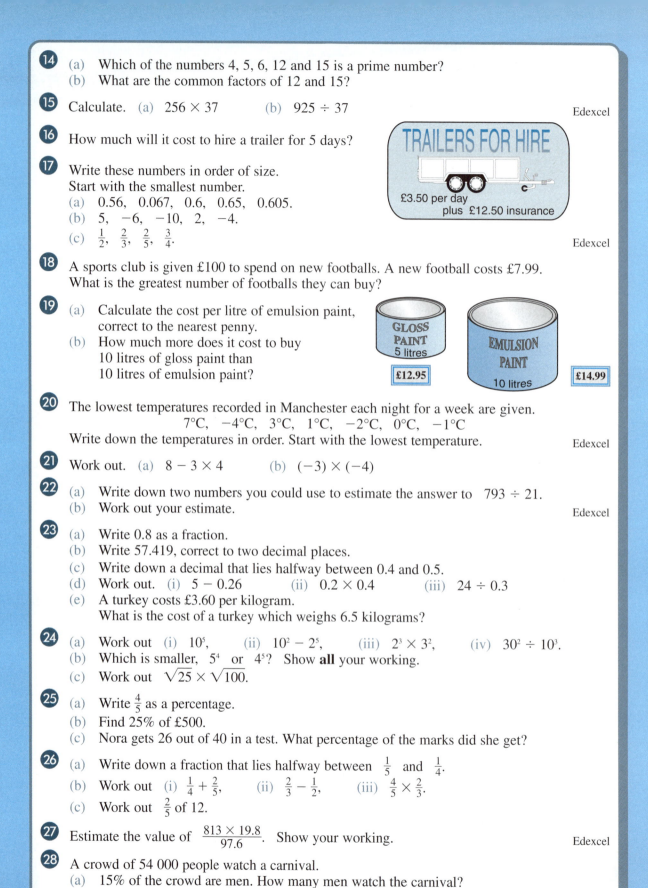

£3.50 per day
plus £12.50 insurance

18 A sports club is given £100 to spend on new footballs. A new football costs £7.99.
What is the greatest number of footballs they can buy?

19 (a) Calculate the cost per litre of emulsion paint, correct to the nearest penny.
(b) How much more does it cost to buy 10 litres of gloss paint than 10 litres of emulsion paint?

GLOSS PAINT 5 litres £12.95
EMULSION PAINT 10 litres £14.99

20 The lowest temperatures recorded in Manchester each night for a week are given.
7°C, −4°C, 3°C, 1°C, −2°C, 0°C, −1°C
Write down the temperatures in order. Start with the lowest temperature.
Edexcel

21 Work out. (a) $8 - 3 \times 4$ (b) $(-3) \times (-4)$

22 (a) Write down two numbers you could use to estimate the answer to $793 \div 21$.
(b) Work out your estimate.
Edexcel

23 (a) Write 0.8 as a fraction.
(b) Write 57.419, correct to two decimal places.
(c) Write down a decimal that lies halfway between 0.4 and 0.5.
(d) Work out. (i) $5 - 0.26$ (ii) 0.2×0.4 (iii) $24 \div 0.3$
(e) A turkey costs £3.60 per kilogram.
What is the cost of a turkey which weighs 6.5 kilograms?

24 (a) Work out (i) 10^5, (ii) $10^2 - 2^5$, (iii) $2^3 \times 3^2$, (iv) $30^2 \div 10^3$.
(b) Which is smaller, 5^4 or 4^5? Show **all** your working.
(c) Work out $\sqrt{25} \times \sqrt{100}$.

25 (a) Write $\frac{4}{5}$ as a percentage.
(b) Find 25% of £500.
(c) Nora gets 26 out of 40 in a test. What percentage of the marks did she get?

26 (a) Write down a fraction that lies halfway between $\frac{1}{5}$ and $\frac{1}{4}$.
(b) Work out (i) $\frac{1}{4} + \frac{2}{5}$, (ii) $\frac{2}{3} - \frac{1}{2}$, (iii) $\frac{4}{5} \times \frac{2}{3}$.
(c) Work out $\frac{2}{5}$ of 12.

27 Estimate the value of $\frac{813 \times 19.8}{97.6}$. Show your working.
Edexcel

28 A crowd of 54 000 people watch a carnival.
(a) 15% of the crowd are men. How many men watch the carnival?
(b) Two-thirds of the crowd are children. How many children watch the carnival?

29 (a) Given that $59 \times 347 = 20\,473$, find the exact value of $\frac{20\,473}{590}$.
(b) Write 4×10^5 as an ordinary number.

30 Simon spent $\frac{1}{3}$ of his pocket money on a computer game.
He spent $\frac{1}{4}$ of his pocket money on a ticket for a football match.
Work out the fraction of his pocket money that he had left. *Edexcel*

31 On average, Nick walks 18 000 steps every day.
He walks 1 mile approximately every 3500 steps.
Work out an estimate for the average distance, in miles, that Nick walks **in one year**. *Edexcel*

32 (a) Diesel costs £0.95 per litre in England. Calculate the cost of 45 litres of diesel.
(b) In France, diesel is 20% cheaper than in England.
Calculate the cost of 45 litres of diesel in France.

33 Mr Smithson insures the contents of his house.
He has to pay £2.10 per £1000 of the value of the contents.
His house contents are valued at £26 500. Calculate how much his insurance costs. *Edexcel*

34 David's foot is 28 cm in length, correct to the nearest centimetre.
What is the minimum length of David's foot?

35 Two lettuces and three cucumbers cost £3.10. Cucumbers cost 64p each.
How much does a lettuce cost?

36 Enzo makes pizzas. One day he makes 36 pizzas. He charges £2.45 for each pizza.
(a) Work out the total amount he charges for 36 pizzas.

Rosa prepares the ingredients for pizzas.
She uses cheese, topping and dough in the ratio 2 : 3 : 5. Rosa uses 70 grams of dough.
(b) Work out the number of grams of cheese and the number of grams of topping Rosa uses. *Edexcel*

37 The price of a box of chocolates is £4.32. There are 24 chocolates in the box.
(a) Work out the cost of **one** chocolate.

18 of the chocolates in a box are milk chocolates.
(b) Work out 18 as a percentage of 24. *Edexcel*

38 Three cups of tea cost £2.85. How much will five cups of tea cost?

39 It costs £1.20 to buy a melon on Tuesday. On Wednesday it costs 15% **more**.
How much does it cost to buy a melon on Wednesday?

40 (a) Conrad cycles 24 km in $1\frac{1}{2}$ hours. What is his cycling speed in kilometres per hour?
(b) Cas cycles 24 km at 15 km/h. She sets off at 0930. At what time does she finish?

41 Work out (a) $\frac{2}{5} + \frac{3}{8}$, (b) $5\frac{2}{3} - 2\frac{3}{4}$. *Edexcel*

42 A box of screws contains 250 screws, to the nearest 10.
(a) What is the smallest possible number of screws in the box?
(b) What is the largest possible number of screws in the box?

43 The prime factors of a certain number are $2^3 \times 3 \times 11$. What is the number? *Edexcel*

44 Write $\dfrac{5^3 \times 5^3}{5^2}$ as a single power of 5.

45 Jack shares £180 between his two children Ruth and Ben.
The ratio of Ruth's share to Ben's share is 5 : 4.
(a) Work out how much each child is given.

Ben then gives 10% of his share to Ruth.
(b) Work out the percentage of the £180 that Ruth now has. *Edexcel*

46 (a) Write as a product of its prime factors: (i) 72, (ii) 96.
(b) Hence, find the least common multiple of 72 and 96.

Number Calculator Paper

Section Review

You may use a calculator for this exercise.

1   **54 327 PEOPLE WATCHED A CONCERT**
(a) Write 54 327 to the nearest thousand.
(b) Write down the value of the 5 in the number 54 327.
Edexcel

2 (a) List these numbers in order, smallest first.

| 13 | 5 | −7 | 0 | −1 |

(b) What is the difference between the largest number and the smallest number in your list?

3 Christine buys a calculator costing £5.95, a pencil case costing £1.62, a ruler costing 25p and two pens costing 48p each.
She pays with a £10 note. How much change should she get from her £10 note?
Edexcel

4 Isaac buys 180 grams of sweets from the Pic 'n' Mix selection.
The price of the sweets is 65p per 100 g.
How much does he have to pay?

5 In a long jump event Hanniah jumped the following distances.
    5.15 m   4.95 m   5.20 m   5.02 m   5.10 m
(a) Write down the shortest distance Hanniah jumped.
(b) Write these distances in order, shortest first.

6 Some of the rail services from Poole to Waterloo are shown.

Poole	0544	0602	—	0640	—	0740	0825	0846
Bournemouth	0558	0616	—	0654	0715	0754	0839	0900
Southampton	0634	0655	0714	0738	0754	0838	0908	0938
Eastleigh	0646	—	—	0750	—	0852	—	0951
Waterloo	0804	0810	0844	0901	0908	1005	1018	1112

(a) Sid arrives at Bournemouth station at 0830.
What is the time of the next train to Eastleigh?
(b) Paul catches the 0654 from Bournemouth to Southampton.
How many minutes does the journey take?

7 The diagram shows the measuring scale on a petrol tank.
The petrol tank holds 28 litres when full.
A litre of petrol cost 86.4 pence.
Work out the cost of the petrol which has to be added to the tank so that it is full.

Edexcel

8 (a) Write $\frac{13}{20}$ as a decimal.
(b) In a spelling test Lara scores 13 out of 20.
What is Lara's score as a percentage?

9 Work out   (a) $\frac{3}{5}$ of 185,   (b) 12% of £9.50.
Edexcel

10 Bruce buys two packets of baby wipes on special offer.
Calculate the actual cost of each baby wipe.

40 BABY WIPES
£2.24

Special Offer
BUY ONE GET ONE FREE

11. A jacket is 70% wool and 30% nylon.

    (a) Write 70% as a decimal.

    (b) Write 30% as a fraction.
        Give your answer in its simplest form.

    (c) Write down the ratio of wool to nylon.

    Edexcel

12. Bertie has to work out $4.2 \times 4.9 \times 31$. He uses a calculator and gets 6379.8
    (a) By rounding each number to one significant figure check Bertie's answer.
        Show all your working.
    (b) What is the mistake in Bertie's answer?

13. (a) Write $\frac{7}{9}$ as a decimal. Give your answer correct to two decimal places.

    (b) Write 33%, 0.3, $\frac{8}{25}$ and $\frac{1}{3}$ in order of size, smallest first.

14. Cheri is paid a basic rate of £6.40 per hour for a 35-hour week.
    Overtime is paid at $1\frac{1}{2}$ times the basic rate.
    Last week she worked 41 hours. Calculate her pay for last week.

15.

    Frances sees three different advertisements for jeans.
    Work out the cost of the jeans in each advertisement.

    Edexcel

16. Jacob is 3.7 kg heavier than Isaac. The sum of their weights is 44.5 kg. How heavy is Jacob?

17. To make squash, orange juice and water is mixed in the ratio of 1 : 6.
    How much orange juice is needed to make 35 litres of squash?

18. Work out the value of $\sqrt{46} - 2.5^2$, correct to one significant figure.

    Edexcel

19. Mrs Joy's electricity meter was read on 1st March and 1st June.
    On 1st March the reading was 3 2 4 5 7   On 1st June the reading was 3 2 9 3 1
    (a) How many units of electricity have been used?

    Her electricity bill for this period includes a fixed charge of £11.58 and the cost of the units used at 9.36 pence per unit.
    (b) Calculate the total cost of electricity for this period.

20. A student bought a pair of sunglasses in the USA. He paid $35.50.
    In England, an identical pair of sunglasses costs £26.99. The exchange rate is £1 = $1.42.
    In which country were the sunglasses cheaper, and by how much?

    Edexcel

21. Fred won a prize of £12 000.
    He put some of the money in a Building Society.
    He put the rest of the money in the Post Office.
    The money was put in the Building Society and Post Office in the ratio 2 : 3.
    (a) Calculate the amount of money put in the Building Society.

    After a number of years the money put in the Building Society had increased by 9%.
    (b) Calculate the amount of money Fred then had in the Building Society.

    After the same number of years the money Fred had put in the Post Office had increased by an eighth.
    (c) Calculate the increase in the amount of money in the Post Office.

    Edexcel

22 Wayne invited 96 people to an engagement party.
Only 60 of the people invited came to the party.
Express 60 as a percentage of 96. *Edexcel*

23 (a) Write the following fractions as decimals, writing all the figures shown on your calculator.
(i) $\frac{9}{10}$ (ii) $\frac{45}{51}$
(b) Work out a fraction that is between $\frac{9}{10}$ and $\frac{45}{51}$ in size. *Edexcel*

24 Harvey lives 3 kilometres from school. He walks to school at an average speed of 5 km/h.
The school day starts at 0900.
What is the latest time Harvey can leave home and still get to school on time?

25 Evaluate $\frac{(23.4 + 35.6) \times 5.7}{200.3 \times (16.2 - 8.15)}$. *Edexcel*

26 In England, a jar of **extra fruity** apricot jam weighs 454 g and costs 89p.
In France, a jar of **extra fruity** apricot jam weighs 681 g and costs 1.84 euros.
   £1 = 1.58 euros.
In which country is the jam better value for money? You must show all your working.

27 There are 12 inches in 1 foot. There are 3 feet in 1 yard. There are 2.54 centimetres in 1 inch.
Express 1 metre in yards. Give your answer correct to 3 decimal places. *Edexcel*

28 Verity and Jean share £126 in the ratio 5 : 3.
Work out how much money Verity receives. *Edexcel*

29 A caravan is for sale at £7200. Stuart buys the caravan on credit.
The credit terms are:

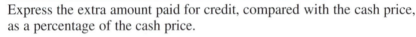

deposit 25% of sale price and 36 monthly payments of £175.

Express the extra amount paid for credit, compared with the cash price,
as a percentage of the cash price.

30 The selling price of a computer is the **list price** plus VAT at $17\frac{1}{2}$%.
The **list price** of a computer is £786. Work out the selling price of the computer. *Edexcel*

31 £1 can buy 1.54 euros. £1 can buy 1.37 dollars.
How many dollars can be bought with 1000 euros?

32 Find the **simple** interest on £3500 invested for 3 years at 4% per year. *Edexcel*

33 (a) What is the reciprocal of 0.25?
(b) Work out $\frac{3.2^2}{\sqrt{0.04}}$.

34 (a) Place the following numbers in order, largest first: $\sqrt{6.9}$ 2.58 1.6^2 $2\frac{4}{7}$
(b) (i) Calculate $\frac{612 \times 29.6}{81.3 - 18.9}$.
   (ii) Use approximations to show that your answer is about right. Show your working.

35 (a) Express 108 as the product of powers of its prime factors.
(b) Find the highest common factor of 108 and 24. *Edexcel*

36 In 2004, Ashley's council tax bill was £965.40.
In 2005, Ashley's council tax bill was 6.8% more than in 2004.
In 2006, Ashley's council tax bill was 4.9% more than in 2005.
Calculate Ashley's council tax bill in 2006.
Give your answer to a suitable degree of accuracy.

37 $p = 3^2 \times 5 \times 7$ and $q = 2 \times 3 \times 5^2$. Find the least common multiple of p and q.

SECTION 12 — Introduction to Algebra

What you need to know

- You should be able to write **algebraic expressions**.
  - **Eg 1** An expression for the cost of 6 pens at n pence each is $6n$ pence.
  - **Eg 2** An expression for 2 pence more than n pence is $n + 2$ pence.
- Be able to **simplify expressions** by collecting **like terms** together.
  - **Eg 3** (a) $2d + 3d = 5d$ (b) $3x + 2 - x + 4 = 2x + 6$ (c) $x + 2x + x^2 = 3x + x^2$
- Be able to **multiply expressions** together.
  - **Eg 4** (a) $2a \times a = 2a^2$ (b) $y \times y \times y = y^3$ (c) $3m \times 2n = 6mn$
- Recall and use these properties of powers:
  Powers of the same base are **added** when terms are **multiplied**.
  Powers of the same base are **subtracted** when terms are **divided**.

  $$a^m \times a^n = a^{m+n}$$
  $$a^m \div a^n = a^{m-n}$$

  - **Eg 5** (a) $x^3 \times x^2 = x^5$ (b) $a^5 \div a^2 = a^3$
- Be able to **multiply out brackets**.
  - **Eg 6** (a) $2(x + 5) = 2x + 10$ (b) $x(x - 5) = x^2 - 5x$
  - (c) $(x + 2)(x + 5) = x^2 + 5x + 2x + 10 = x^2 + 7x + 10$
- Be able to **factorise expressions**.
  - **Eg 7** (a) $3x - 6 = 3(x - 2)$ (b) $m^2 + 5m = m(m + 5)$

Exercise 12

1. A calculator costs £9.
   Write an expression for the cost of k calculators.

2. Godfrey is 5 years older than Mary.
   Write an expression for Godfrey's age when Mary is t years old.

3. Simplify. (a) $q + q + q + q$ (b) $7x + 3y + 2x - 2y$ *Edexcel*

4. A cup of coffee costs x pence and a cup of tea costs y pence.
   Write an expression for the cost of 3 cups of coffee and 2 cups of tea.

5. Simplify. (a) $m + 2m + 3m$ (b) $2m + 2 - m$ (c) $m \times m \times m$

6. Simplify (a) $5x + 3x - x$, (b) $4y - 3 + 3y - 2$. *Edexcel*

7. Write an expression, in terms of x, for the sum of the angles in this shape.

8. A muffin costs $d + 3$ pence.
   Write an expression for the cost of 5 muffins.

9. Simplify $5x + 3y - y + 2x$. *Edexcel*

10. Simplify (a) $5a \times 2a$, (b) $3g \times 2h$, (c) $6k \div 3$, (d) $3m \div m$.

11 Lisa packs pencils in boxes. She packs 12 pencils in each box. Lisa packs x boxes of pencils.
  (a) Write an expression, in terms of x, for the number of pencils Lisa packs.

  Lisa also packs pens in boxes. She packs 10 pens into each box. Lisa packs y boxes of pens.
  (b) Write an expression, in terms of x and y, for the **total** number of pens and pencils Lisa packs.

12 Pete thought of 4 different algebraic expressions.
  (a) Add these 4 expressions.
      Give your answer in its simplest form.
  (b) Use two of Pete's expressions to make this statement true.
      .... is twice ....

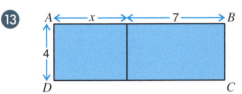

13 The diagram shows a rectangle, $ABCD$.
The measurements on the diagram are in centimetres.
Write down an expression, in terms of x, for the area of the rectangle $ABCD$.

14 Which of these algebraic expressions are equivalent?

$a + a$	$2(a + 1)$	$2a + 1$	$2a + 2$	a^3
a^2	$a + a + 1$	$2a$	$a + a + a$	$a \times a$

15 (a) Simplify (i) $2x + 3 + x$, (ii) $2x + y - x + y$.
  (b) Multiply out (i) $2(x + 3)$, (ii) $x(x - 1)$.
  (c) Multiply out and simplify (i) $2(x - 1) - 3$, (ii) $7 + 3(2 + x)$.
  (d) Factorise (i) $2a - 6$, (ii) $x^2 + 2x$.

16 (a) Simplify. (i) $x + x + x$ (ii) $2a + 4b + a - 2b$ (iii) $3(a + 2)$
  (b) Expand and simplify. $2(x - 1) + 3(2x + 1)$

17 (a) Ken works x hours a week for £y per hour.
      Write an expression for the amount he earns each week.
  (b) Sue works 5 hours less than Ken each week and earns £y per hour.
      Write an expression for the amount Sue earns each week.

18 (a) Simplify $2ab + 3a - 2b + b - 5a + ab$.
  (b) Multiply out and simplify $3(2x + 3) + 2(5 + x)$.

19 Ahmed and Hussein are two brothers. Ahmed is older than Hussein.
Given that Ahmed's age is $(5x - 4)$ years and Hussein's age is $(2x + 1)$ years, write down an expression, in terms of x, for how much older Ahmed is than Hussein.
Simplify your answer.

20 Simplify. (a) $y^3 \times y^2$ (b) $x^6 \div x^3$ (c) $\dfrac{z^4 \times z}{z^3}$

21 (a) Multiply out $t^2(t^3 - t^4)$.
  (b) Multiply out and simplify $3(2a + 6) - 2(3a - 6)$.

22 (a) Simplify (i) $5 - 3(2n - 1)$, (ii) $3(2x + 3) - 2(5 + x)$.
  (b) Multiply out and simplify $(p - 3)(p + 4)$.

23 Simplify. (a) $a \times a \times a \times a$ (b) $b \times b^3$ (c) $\dfrac{c^5}{c^2}$ (d) $\dfrac{d^3 \times d^5}{d^4}$

24 (a) Factorise $4x + 6$.
  (b) Expand (i) $3(2y - 3)$, (ii) $x(x^2 - 2x)$, (iii) $a(a + b)$.
  (c) Simplify $2x^2 - x(1 + x)$.

25 Expand and simplify $(x - 6)(x + 4)$.

SECTION 13 — Solving Equations

What you need to know

- The solution of an equation is the value of the unknown letter that fits the equation.
- You should be able to solve simple equations by **inspection**.

  Eg 1 (a) $a + 2 = 5$ (b) $m - 3 = 7$ (c) $2x = 10$ (d) $\frac{t}{4} = 3$

  $a = 3$ $m = 10$ $x = 5$ $t = 12$

- Be able to solve simple problems by **working backwards**.

  Eg 2 I think of a number, multiply it by 3 and add 4. The answer is 19.

  x → multiply by 3 → add 4 → Answer 19

  5 ← divide by 3 ← 15 ← subtract 4 ← 19

  The number I thought of is 5.

- Be able to use the **balance method** to solve equations.

  Eg 3 Solve these equations.

  (a) $d - 13 = -5$ (b) $-4a = 20$ (c) $5 - 4n = -1$

  $d = -5 + 13$ $a = \frac{20}{-4}$ $-4n = -6$

  $d = 8$ $a = -5$ $n = 1.5$

Exercise 13

1 What number should be put in the box to make each of these statements correct?

(a) ☐ $- 6 = 9$ (b) $2 +$ ☐ $= 11$ (c) $4 \times$ ☐ $= 20$ (d) $\frac{☐}{5} = 3$

2 Solve these equations.

(a) $7 + x = 12$ (b) $5 - x = 3$ (c) $\frac{x}{2} = 7$ (d) $3x = 21$

3 Lindi thought of a number. She multiplied the number by 5. Her answer was 30. What number did Lindi think of?

Edexcel

4 The diagram shows a mathematical rule. Copy and complete the table.

Input → × 2 → + 3 → Output

Input	3		−2
Output		13	

5 (a) I think of a number, add 3, and then multiply by 2. The answer is 16. What is my number?

(b) I think of a number, double it and then subtract 3. The answer is 5. What is my number?

6 Solve these equations.

(a) $3x - 7 = 23$ (b) $4 + 3x = 19$ (c) $5x - 9 = 11$ (d) $5 - 7x = 47$

7 Solve these equations.

(a) $3x + 5 = 2$ (b) $4x = 2$ (c) $4x + 1 = 23$ (d) $5x + 1 = -3$

SECTION 14 — Further Equations

What you need to know

- To solve an equation you need to find the numerical value of the letter, by ending up with **one letter** on one side of the equation and a **number** on the other side of the equation.

- You should be able to solve equations with unknowns on both sides of the equals sign.

  Eg 1 Solve $3x + 1 = x + 7$.
  $3x = x + 6$
  $2x = 6$
  $x = 3$

- Be able to solve equations which include brackets.

  Eg 2 Solve $2(x - 3) = 4$.
  $2x - 6 = 4$
  $2x = 10$
  $x = 5$

- You should be able to solve equations using a **trial and improvement** method.
  The value of the unknown letter is improved until the required degree of accuracy is obtained.

  Eg 3 Use a trial and improvement method to find a solution to the equation $x^3 + x = 40$, correct to one decimal place.

x	$x^3 + x$	Comment
3	$27 + 3 = 30$	Too small
4	$64 + 4 = 68$	Too big
3.5	$42.8... + 3.5 = 46.3...$	Too big
3.3	$35.9... + 3.3 = 39.2...$	Too small
3.35	$37.5... + 3.35 = 40.9...$	Too big

  For accuracy to 1 d.p. check the second decimal place. The solution lies between 3.3 and 3.35.

  $x = 3.3$, correct to 1 d.p.

- You should be able to write, or form, equations using the information given in a problem.

Exercise 14

1 Solve these equations. (a) $3 + x = 7$ (b) $3 - x = 4$ (c) $3x = 15$ (d) $\frac{x}{3} = 7$

2 Pete thought of a number. He multiplied it by 3.
Then he subtracted 5 from the result.
The answer was 7.
Find the number Pete first thought of.
Edexcel

3 x, y and z represent different numbers, such that:
$x + x + x = 21$, $x + y + y = 17$ and $x + y + z = 9$
Find the values of x, y and z.

4 Solve $5x - 3 = 2x + 15$.
Edexcel

5 Solve the equations (a) $3x - 7 = x + 15$, (b) $5(x - 2) = 20$.

6. Solve these equations.
   (a) $7x + 4 = 60$
   (b) $3x - 7 = -4$
   (c) $2(x + 3) = -2$
   (d) $3x - 4 = 1 + x$

7. Solve the equations
   (a) $2p - 3 = 7$,
   (b) $6 - q = 7$,
   (c) $3r - 4 = 7r + 2$.
   Edexcel

8. Solve these equations.
   (a) $2x + 5 = 2$
   (b) $2(x - 1) = 3$
   (c) $5 - 2x = 3x + 2$
   (d) $2(3 + x) = 9$

9. Solve.
   (a) $5t - 1 = 24$
   (b) $4x + 3 = 2x + 10$
   (c) $7y + 21 = 3y - 3$
   Edexcel

10. The lengths of these rods are given, in centimetres, in terms of n.

     n 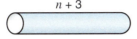 $n + 3$ $2n - 1$

    (a) Write an expression, in terms of n, for the total length of the rods.
    (b) The total length of the rods is 30 cm.
        By forming an equation, find the value of n.

11. Mandy buys a small box of chocolates and a large box of chocolates.
    The diagram shows the number of chocolates in each box.
    Altogether there are 47 chocolates.
    By forming an equation, find the number
    of chocolates in the larger box.

     n chocolates $2n + 5$ chocolates

12. A cracker costs n pence.
    A party hat costs 7 pence less than a cracker.
    (a) Write an expression for the cost of a party hat.
    (b) The cost of 10 crackers and 5 party hats is £4.45
        By forming an equation in n find the cost of a party hat.

13. Solve these equations.
    (a) $3y + 7 = 28$
    (b) $2(3p + 2) = 19$
    (c) $3t - 4 = 5t - 10$
    Edexcel

14. Solve.
    (a) $4a + 3 = 9$
    (b) $5b - 7 = 2b + 5$
    (c) $3(c - 6) = 10 - 2c$
    Edexcel

15. Solve the equation $5(x - 3) = 2x$.

16. Solve these equations.
    (a) $\frac{x}{3} = -7$
    (b) $5x - 3 = 7$
    (c) $2(y + 5) = 3$
    (d) $z + 7 = 3 - 4z$

17. Solve the equations
    (a) $5(2p - 3) = 50$,
    (b) $\frac{16 - q}{3} = 3$.
    Edexcel

18.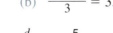

    The diagram shows two straight lines AB and CD. Each line is cut into sections.
    The length, in centimetres, of each section is shown in the diagram.
    (a) Write down, in terms of d, (i) the length of AB, (ii) the length of CD.

    The length of AB is equal to the length of CD.
    (b) (i) Write down an equation in d.
        (ii) Solve your equation to find the value of d.
    Edexcel

19. Solve $4(2x + 1) = 2(3 - x)$.
    Edexcel

20. The equation $x^3 - 5x = 38$ has a solution between 3 and 4.
    Use a trial and improvement method to find this solution.
    Give your answer correct to 1 decimal place.
    You must show **all** your working.
    Edexcel

SECTION 15 Formulae

What you need to know

- An **expression** is just an answer using letters and numbers.
  A **formula** is an algebraic rule. It always has an equals sign.
- You should be able to **write simple formulae**.

  Eg 1 A packet of crisps weighs 25 grams.
  Write a formula for the total weight, W grams, of n packets of crisps.
  $W = 25n$

  Eg 2 Start with t, add 5 and then multiply by 3.
  The result is p.
  Write a formula for p in terms of t.
  $p = 3(t + 5)$

- Be able to **substitute** values into expressions and formulae.

  Eg 3 (a) Find the value of
  $4x - y$ when
  $x = 5$ and $y = 7$.
  $4x - y = 4 \times 5 - 7$
  $= 20 - 7$
  $= 13$

  (b) $A = pq - r$
  Find the value of
  A when $p = 2$,
  $q = -2$ and $r = 3$.
  $A = pq - r$
  $A = 2 \times (-2) - 3$
  $A = -4 - 3$
  $A = -7$

  (c) $M = 2n^2$
  Find the value of
  M when $n = 3$.
  $M = 2n^2$
  $M = 2 \times 3^2$
  $M = 2 \times 9$
  $M = 18$

- Be able to **rearrange** a simple formula to make another letter (variable) the subject.

  Eg 4 $y = 2x + 5$. Make x the subject of the formula.
  $y = 2x + 5$
  Take 5 from both sides. $y - 5 = 2x$
  Divide both sides by 2. $\dfrac{y - 5}{2} = x$. So, $x = \dfrac{y - 5}{2}$

Exercise 15

Do not use a calculator for questions 1 to 14.

1 What is the value of $a - 3b$ when $a = 10$ and $b = 2$?

2 What is the value of $2x + y$ when $x = -3$ and $y = 5$?

3 $P = 2l + 2w$. $l = 12$ and $w = 8$. Work out the value of P. *Edexcel*

4 Given that $m = -3$ and $n = 5$, find the value of
(a) $m + n$, (b) $m - n$, (c) $n - m$, (d) mn.

5 $H = ab - c$. Find the value of H when $a = 2$, $b = -5$ and $c = 3$.

6 The cost, in £, to hire a bicycle is given by:

Cost = 3 × Number of hours + 2

Calculate the cost of hiring two bicycles for 5 hours.

7 $L = 5(p + q)$. Find the value of L when $p = 2$ and $q = -4$.

8 A pie costs 65 pence. Pam buys n pies. The total cost is C pence.
Write down a formula connecting C and n. Edexcel

9 $A = b - cd$. Find the value of A when $b = -3$, $c = 2$ and $d = 4$.

10 What is the value of $10y^2$ when $y = 3$?

11 What is the value of $3x^3$ when $x = 2$?

12 $T = ab^2$. Find the value of T when $a = 4$ and $b = -5$.

13 $P = Q^2 - 2Q$. Find the value of P when $Q = -3$. Edexcel

14 This is how to work out the amount of meat a dog needs to eat each day.

> Find what the dog weighs and multiply by 0.04

(a) Use m for the amount of meat and w for what the dog weighs.
Write a formula for m in terms of w.

Scamp is a dog that weighs 30 kg.
(b) How much meat does he need to eat each day? Edexcel

15 A pen costs 25 pence. A pencil costs 10 pence.
Louisa buys x pens and y pencils. The total cost is C pence.
(a) Write a formula for C in terms of x and y.
(b) Work out the value of y when $C = 250$ and $x = 6$. Edexcel

16 (a) Write, in symbols, the rule:

> "To find y, double x and add 1."

(b) Use your rule from part (a) to calculate the value of x when $y = 9$. Edexcel

17 The cost of using an appliance is calculated by the formula:

> cost = number of kilowatts × number of hours × 7 pence

Find the cost of using
(a) a 3 kilowatt heater for 5 hours,
(b) a 0.36 kilowatt TV set for 50 hours. Edexcel

18 This rule is used to change miles into kilometres.

> Multiply the number of miles by 8 and then divide by 5

(a) Use the rule to change 25 miles into kilometres.
(b) Using K for the number of kilometres and M for the number of miles write a formula for K in terms of M.
(c) Use your formula to find the value of M when $K = 60$.

19 $c = y - mx$. Calculate the value of c when $y = 4.95$, $m = -0.75$ and $x = 3$. Edexcel

20 A formula is given as $c = 3t - 5$. Rearrange the formula to give t in terms of c.

21 $s = \frac{1}{2}(u + v)t$. Work out the value of s when $u = 10$, $v = -25$ and $t = 0.5$. Edexcel

22 Rearrange the formula $n = 3 + mp$ to make m the subject.

23 $m = 3(n - 17)$. Find the value of n when $m = -9$.

24 Make r the subject of the formula $p = \frac{5r}{s}$.

25 You are given the formula $v = u + at$.
(a) Find v when $u = 17$, $a = -8$ and $t = 3$.
(b) Rearrange the formula to give a in terms of v, u and t.

SECTION 16 Sequences

What you need to know

- A **sequence** is a list of numbers made according to some rule.
  The numbers in a sequence are called **terms**.

- You should be able to draw and continue number sequences represented by patterns of shapes.

  Eg 1 This pattern represents the sequence: 3, 5, 7, ...

- Be able to continue a sequence by following a given rule.

  Eg 2 The sequence 2, 7, 22, ... is made using the rule:

  > Multiply the last number by 3, then add 1.

  The next term in the sequence = $(22 \times 3) + 1 = 66 + 1 = 67$

- Be able to find a rule, and then use it, to continue a sequence.

  > **To continue a sequence:**
  > 1. Work out the rule to get from one term to the next.
  > 2. Apply the same rule to find further terms in the sequence.

  Eg 3 Describe the rule used to make the following sequences.
  Then use the rule to find the next term of each sequence.
  (a) 5, 8, 11, 14, ...   Rule: add 3 to last term.   Next term: 17.
  (b) 2, 4, 8, 16, ...   Rule: multiply last term by 2.   Next term: 32.
  (c) 1, 1, 2, 3, 5, 8, ... Rule: add the last two terms.   Next term: 13.

- Special sequences   **Square numbers:**   1, 4, 9, 16, 25, ...
                      Triangular numbers: 1, 3, 6, 10, 15, ...

- A number sequence which increases (or decreases) by the same amount from one term to the next is called a **linear sequence**.
  The sequence: 2, 8, 14, 20, 26, ... has a **common difference** of 6.

- You should be able to find an expression for the n th term of a linear sequence.

  Eg 4 Find the n th term of the sequence: 3, 5, 7, 9, ...
  The sequence is linear, common difference = 2.
  To find the n th term add one to the multiples of 2.
  So, the n th term is $2n + 1$.

Exercise 16

1 Write down the next two terms in each of these linear sequences.
   (a) 1, 5, 9, 13, 17, ...   (b) 50, 46, 42, 38, 34, ...

2 Here are the first five terms of a number sequence.   3   8   13   18   23
   (a) Write down the next **two** terms of the sequence.
   (b) Explain how you found your answer.
   (c) Explain why 387 is **not** a term of the sequence.
                                                                    Edexcel

3 The diagrams show patterns made out of sticks.

  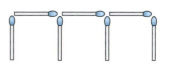

    Pattern number 1   Pattern number 2   Pattern number 3

(a) Draw a diagram to show pattern number 4.

The table can be used to show the number of sticks needed for a pattern.

Pattern number	1	2	3	4	5	6	7
Number of sticks	3	5					

(b) Copy and complete the table.
(c) (i) Work out the number of sticks needed for pattern number 15.
    (ii) Explain how you obtained your answer. *Edexcel*

4 What is the next number in each of these sequences?
(a) 1, 2, 5, 10, …   (b) 1, 3, 9, 27, …   (c) 1, $\frac{1}{2}$, $\frac{1}{4}$, $\frac{1}{8}$, …

5 Here are the first four terms in a sequence: 6, 12, 18, 24.
(a) (i) Write down the 5th term in the sequence.
    (ii) Explain how you worked out your answer.
(b) Which term in the sequence is equal to 72? *Edexcel*

6 (a) The rule for a sequence of numbers is:

> ADD THE TWO PREVIOUS NUMBERS AND THEN MULTIPLY BY 2

Write down the next two numbers in the sequence: 1, 1, 4, 10, …
(b) The first eight numbers in a different sequence of numbers are:
    3, 7, 4, 8, 5, 9, 6, 10, …
Write down the next two numbers in the sequence. *Edexcel*

7 The first six terms of a sequence are shown. 1, 4, 5, 9, 14, 23, …
Write down the next two terms.

8 A sequence begins: 1, 6, 10, 8, … The rule to continue the sequence is:
double the difference between the last two numbers.
Ravi says if you continue the sequence it will end in 0. Is he correct? Explain your answer.

9 The first three patterns in a sequence are shown.

         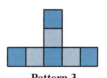

    Pattern 1   Pattern 2   Pattern 3

(a) How many squares are in pattern 20? Explain how you found your answer.
(b) Write an expression for the number of squares in the n th pattern.

10 Here are the first four terms of a number sequence: 3, 7, 11, 15.
(a) Write down the next two terms of the sequence.
(b) Write down an expression, in terms of n, for the n th term of the sequence. *Edexcel*

11 Find the n th term of the following sequences.
(a) 5, 7, 9, 11, …   (b) 1, 5, 9, 13, …

12 Marco writes down a number sequence. He starts at 120.
Each time he subtracts 12 to get the next number in the sequence.
(a) Write down the first 5 numbers in the sequence.
(b) Write down an expression for the n th number in the sequence. *Edexcel*

13 (a) Write down the first **three** terms of the sequence whose n th term is given by $n^2 - 4$.
(b) Will the number 60 be in this sequence? Explain your answer.

SECTION 17 Coordinates and Graphs

What you need to know

- **Coordinates** (involving positive and negative numbers) are used to describe the position of a point on a graph.

  Eg 1 The coordinates of A are (4, 1).
  The coordinates of B are (−3, 2).

- The x axis is the line $y = 0$. The y axis is the line $x = 0$.
- The x axis crosses the y axis at the **origin**.
- The graph of a linear function is a straight line.
- You should be able to draw the graph of a straight line.

  Eg 2 Draw the graphs of the following lines.

  (a) $y = 2$ (b) $x = 3$ (c) $y = \frac{1}{2}x + 1$

The graph is a **horizontal** line. All points on the line have y coordinate 2.	The graph is a **vertical** line. All points on the line have x coordinate 3.	Find values for x and y.

  For (c):

x	0	2	4
y	1	2	3

  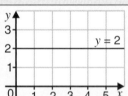
  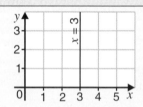
  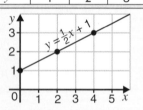

- Be able to draw the graph of a straight line by finding the points where the line crosses the x axis and the y axis.

  Eg 3 Draw the graph of the line $x + 2y = 4$.

  > At the point where a graph crosses:
  > the x axis, $y = 0$,
  > the y axis, $x = 0$.

  When $y = 0$, $x + 0 = 4$, $x = 4$. Plot (4, 0).
  When $x = 0$, $0 + 2y = 4$, $y = 2$. Plot (0, 2).
  A straight line drawn through the points (0, 2) and (4, 0) is the graph of $x + 2y = 4$.

  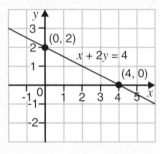

- The equation of the graph of a straight line is of the form $y = mx + c$, where m is the gradient and c is the y-intercept.

  The **gradient** of a line can be found by drawing a right-angled triangle.

  Gradient = $\dfrac{\text{distance up}}{\text{distance along}}$

  Gradients can be positive, zero or negative.

  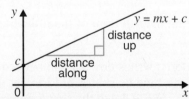

You should be able to:
- interpret the graph of a linear function,
- use the graphs of linear functions to solve equations.

Exercise 17

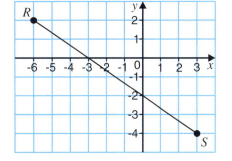

1 The diagram shows the line segment RS.
  (a) Write down the coordinates of points R and S.
  (b) The straight line joining R and S crosses the x axis at T and the y axis at U. Write down the coordinates of T and U.

2 Draw and label x and y axes from −5 to 4.
  (a) On your diagram plot $A(4, 3)$ and $B(-5, -3)$.
  (b) $C(p, -1)$ is on the line segment AB. What is the value of p?

3 (a) On the same diagram draw the lines $y = 2$ and $x = 5$.
  (b) Write down the coordinates of the point where the lines cross.

4 (a) Copy and complete the table of values for $y = 3x - 2$.

x	−1	0	1	2	3
y = 3x − 2					

  (b) Plot your values for x and y. Join your points with a straight line.
  (c) Write down the coordinates of the point where your graph crosses the y axis. *Edexcel*

5 (a) Copy and complete this table of values for $y = 2x + 3$.

x	−3	−2	−1	0	1	2
y		−1				

  (b) Draw the graph of $y = 2x + 3$ for values of x from −3 to 2.
  (c) Use your graph to find (i) the value of y when $x = 1.5$,
                         (ii) the value of x when $y = -0.5$. *Edexcel*

6 (a) On the same axes, draw the graphs of $y = -2$, $y = x$ and $x + y = 5$.
  (b) Which of these lines has a negative gradient?

7 The diagram shows a sketch of the line $2y = 6 - x$.
  (a) Find the coordinates of the points P and Q.
  (b) The line $2y = 6 - x$ goes through $R(-5, m)$. What is the value of m?

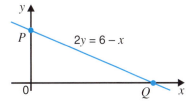

8 Points A, B and C are shown on the grid.
  (a) Write down the equation of the line AB.
  (b) Use the grid to work out the gradient of the line CB.

9 On the same grid draw the graphs of (a) $y = \frac{1}{2}x + 1$, (b) $x = -2$. *Edexcel*

10 (a) Copy and complete the table of values for $2y = 3x - 6$.

x	−2	0	4
y		−3	

  (b) Draw the graph of $2y = 3x - 6$ for values of x from −2 to 4.
  (c) Use your graph to find the value of x when $y = 1.5$.

11 (a) Draw the graph of $5y - 2x = 10$ for values of x from −5 to 5.
  (b) Use your graph to find the value of y when $x = -2$.

SECTION 18 — Using Graphs

What you need to know

- A graph used to change from one quantity into an equivalent quantity is called a **conversion graph**.

  Eg 1 Use 15 kilograms = 33 pounds (lb) to draw a conversion graph for kilograms and pounds.

  Use your graph to find (a) 5 kilograms in pounds, (b) 20 pounds in kilograms.

  The straight line drawn through the points (0, 0) and (33, 15) is the conversion graph for kilograms and pounds.

  Reading from the graph:
  (a) 5 kg = 11 lb
  (b) 20 lb = 9 kg

- **Distance-time graphs** are used to illustrate journeys.

  On a distance-time graph:
  Speed can be calculated from the gradient of a line.
  The faster the speed the steeper the gradient.
  Zero gradient (horizontal line) means zero speed.

  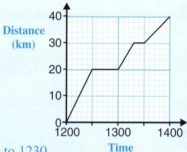

  Eg 2 The graph shows a car journey.
  (a) How many times does the car stop?
  (b) (i) Between what times does the car travel fastest? Explain your answer.
  (ii) What is the speed of the car during this part of the journey?

  (a) Twice
  (b) (i) 1200 to 1230. Steepest gradient.
  (ii) Speed = $\dfrac{\text{Distance}}{\text{Time}} = \dfrac{20\,\text{km}}{\frac{1}{2}\,\text{hour}} = 40\,\text{km/h}$

- You should be able to draw and interpret graphs arising from real-life situations.

Exercise 18

1 The graph shows the temperature of the water in a tank as it is being heated.

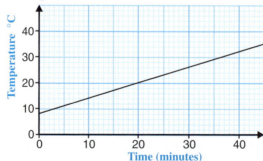

(a) What was the temperature of the water before it was heated?
(b) How long did it take for the water to reach 26°C?
(c) Estimate the number of minutes it will take for the temperature of the water to rise from 32°C to 50°C.

2 This conversion graph can be used to convert between miles and kilometres.

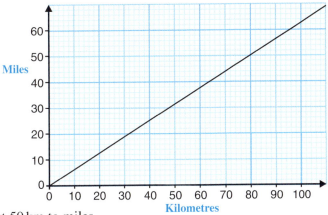

(a) Convert 50 km to miles.
(b) Convert 27 miles to kilometres.
(c) Explain how the information on the graph could be used to convert 10 000 km to miles.
Edexcel

3 (a) Given that 7.4 square metres = 80 square feet, draw a conversion graph for square metres to square feet.
(b) Use your graph to change
  (i) 5 square metres into square feet,
  (ii) 32 square feet into square metres.

4 The graph shows the cost, in pounds, of electricity used by one person.
The cost is made up of a fixed standing charge, plus the cost of the number of units of electricity used.

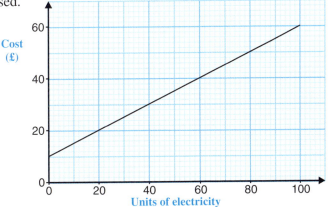

Use the graph to find (a) the standing charge in pounds,
(b) the cost, in pence, of one unit of electricity.
Edexcel

5 Here is part of a travel graph of Siân's journey from her house to the shops and back.

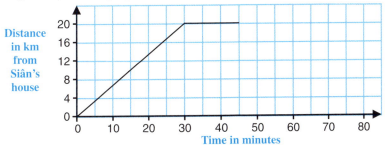

(a) Work out Siân's speed for the first 30 minutes of her journey. Give your answer in km/h.

Siân spends 15 minutes at the shops. She then travels back to her house at 60 km/h.
(b) Copy and complete the travel graph.
Edexcel

6 A salesman is paid a basic amount each month plus commission on sales.
The graph shows how the monthly pay of the salesman depends on his sales.

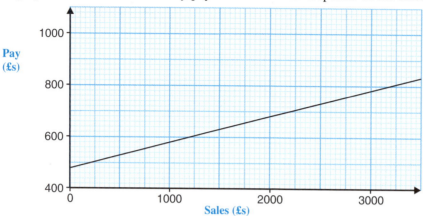

(a) How much is the salesman's monthly basic pay?
(b) How much commission is the salesman paid on £1000 of sales?
(c) Calculate the monthly pay of the salesman when his sales are £5000.

7 Ken and Wendy go from home to their caravan site.
The caravan site is 50 km from their home.
Ken goes on his bike. Wendy drives in her car.
The diagram shows information about the journeys they made.

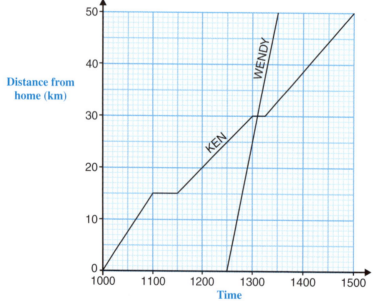

(a) At what time did Wendy pass Ken?
(b) Between which two times was Ken cycling at his greatest speed?
(c) Work out Wendy's average speed for her journey.

Edexcel

8 Ken drives from his home to the city centre.
The graph represents his journey.
(a) How long did Ken take to reach the city centre?
(b) How far from the city centre does Ken live?
(c) What is his average speed for the journey in kilometres per hour?

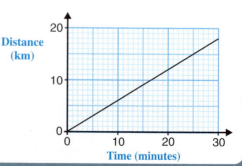

SECTION 19 — Inequalities

What you need to know

- **Inequalities** can be described using words or numbers and symbols.

Sign	Meaning
<	is less than
≤	is less than or equal to

Sign	Meaning
>	is greater than
≥	is greater than or equal to

- Inequalities can be shown on a **number line**.

  Eg 1 This diagram shows the inequality: $-2 < x \leq 3$

  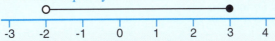

  The circle is: **filled** if the inequality is **included** (i.e. ≤ or ≥),
  not filled if the inequality is **not included** (i.e. < or >).

- **Solving inequalities** means finding the values of x which make the inequality true.

  Eg 2 Solve these inequalities.
  (a) $3x < 6$ (b) $x + 3 \geq 5$ (c) $7a \geq a + 9$
      $x < 2$ $x \geq 2$ $6a \geq 9$
                                                                          $a \geq 1.5$

  Eg 3 Find the integer values of n for which $-1 \leq 2n + 3 < 7$.
  $-1 \leq 2n + 3 < 7$
  $-4 \leq 2n < 4$
  $-2 \leq n < 2$
  Integer values which satisfy the inequality $-1 \leq 2n + 3 < 7$ are: $-2, -1, 0, 1$

Exercise 19

1 Solve these inequalities.
(a) $5x > 15$ (b) $x + 3 \geq 1$ (c) $x - 5 \leq 1$ (d) $3 + 2x > 7$

2 Draw number lines to show each of these inequalities.
(a) $x \geq -2$ (b) $\frac{x}{3} < -1$ (c) $-1 < x \leq 3$ (d) $x \leq -1$ **and** $x > 3$

3 (a) Solve the inequality $3x - 2 \leq 7$.
(b) Show the solution to (a) on a number line.

4 List all the possible integer values of n such that $-3 \leq n < 2$.   *Edexcel*

5 n is a whole number such that $6 < 2n < 13$. List all the possible values of n.   *Edexcel*

6 Solve these inequalities.
(a) $2x \leq 6 - x$ (b) $3x > x + 7$ (c) $5x < 2x - 4$

7 List the values of n, where n is an integer such that:
(a) $-2 \leq 2n < 6$ (b) $-3 < n - 3 \leq -1$ (c) $-5 \leq 2n - 3 < 1$

8 Solve the inequality $7y > 2y - 3$.   *Edexcel*

9 (a) Solve the inequality $5x - 7 < 2x - 1$.
(b) Represent the solution set to part (a) on a number line.   *Edexcel*

SECTION 20 — Quadratic Graphs

What you need to know

- The graph of a **quadratic function** is a **smooth curve**.
- The general equation for a **quadratic function** is
  $y = ax^2 + bx + c$, where a cannot be zero.
  The graph of a quadratic function is symmetrical and has a **maximum** or **minimum** value.

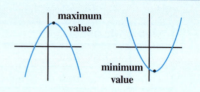

You should be able to:
- **substitute** values into given functions to generate points,
- plot graphs of **quadratic functions**,
- use graphs of quadratic functions to solve equations.

Eg 1 (a) Draw the graph of $y = x^2 - 2x - 5$ for values of x from -2 to 4.
(b) Use your graph to solve the equation $x^2 - 2x - 5 = 0$.

(a)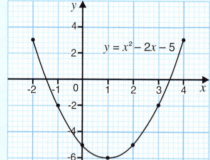

To draw a quadratic graph:
Make a table of values connecting x and y.
Plot the points.
Join the points with a smooth curve.

x	-2	-1	0	1	2	3	4
y	3	-2	-5	-6	-5	-2	3

To solve the equation, read the values of x where the graph of $y = x^2 - 2x - 5$ crosses the x axis ($y = 0$).

(b) $x = -1.4$ and 3.4, correct to one decimal place.

Exercise 20

1 (a) Copy and complete this table of values for $y = x^2 - 2$.

x	-3	-2	-1	0	1	2	3
y		2		-2	-1		7

(b) Draw the graph of $y = x^2 - 2$ for values of x from -3 to 3.
(c) Write down the values of x at the points where the line $y = 3$ crosses your graph.
(d) Write down the values of x where $y = x^2 - 2$ crosses the x axis.

2 (a) Draw the graph of $y = x^2 + x - 2$ for values of x from -2 to 3.
(b) State the minimum value of y.
(c) Use your graph to solve the equation $x^2 + x - 2 = 0$.

3 (a) Copy and complete the table of values for $y = 2x^2$.

x	-3	-2	-1	0	1	2	3
y	18				2	8	

(b) Draw the graph of $y = 2x^2$.
(c) Use your graph to find (i) the value of y when $x = 2.5$,
(ii) the values of x when $y = 12$.

Edexcel

Algebra Non-calculator Paper

Do not use a calculator for this exercise.

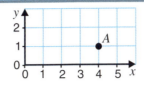

1 What are the coordinates of *A*?

2 A sequence begins 2, 4, 6, …
To continue the sequence use the rule: Add 2 to the last term.
(a) Write down the next term in the sequence.
(b) Explain why the number 99 is not a term in this sequence.

3 In each part, find the output when the input is 12.
(a)
(b)

4 Use this rule to find the number of points a football team has scored.
Points scored = 3 × Number of wins + Number of draws
A team wins 7 games and draws 5. How many points have they scored?

5 Regular pentagons are used to form patterns, as shown.

Pattern 1   Pattern 2   Pattern 3

(a) Draw Pattern 4.
(b) Copy and complete the table.

Pattern number	1	2	3	4
Number of sides	5	8	11	

(c) How many sides has Pattern 5?
(d) Pattern 10 has 32 sides. How many sides has Pattern 11?

6 Find the value of $3a + 2b$ when $a = 5$ and $b = 3$.

7 (a) On graph paper, plot the points $A(-3, -2)$ and $B(1, 4)$.
(b) What are the coordinates of the midpoint of the line segment AB?

8 Here are the first five terms of a number sequence.   1   5   10   16   23
Write down the next **two** terms of the sequence.   *Edexcel*

9 A jam doughnut costs *t* pence.
(a) Write an expression for the cost of 5 jam doughnuts.
A cream doughnut costs 5 pence more than a jam doughnut.
(b) Write an expression for the cost of a cream doughnut.

10 What number should be put in the box to make each of these statements correct?
(a) ☐ − 3 = 7   (b) ☐ + 5 = 9   (c) 3 × ☐ = 6   (d) ☐/3 = 5

11 (a) (i) What is the next term in this sequence?   2, 9, 16, 23, …
(ii) Will the 50th term in the sequence be an odd number or an even number?
Give a reason for your answer.
(b) Another sequence begins   1, 5, 9, 13, 17, …
Describe in words the rule for continuing the sequence.

12 $2n$ represents any even number.
Which of the statements describes the number　(a) n,　(b) $2n + 1$?
　　　　always even　　　always odd　　　could be even or odd

13 Ian thought of a number. He doubled his number and added 5. His answer was 19.
What number did Ian think of?
Edexcel

14 A large envelope costs x pence and a small envelope costs y pence.
Write an expression for the cost of 3 large envelopes and 5 small envelopes.

15 Which of these algebraic expressions are equivalent?

| $2a - a$ | $3a$ | $2(a - 1)$ | $2a + a$ |
| $2a + 1$ | $2a - 2$ | $a + a - 1$ | 2 |

16 Simplify　(a) $7x - 5x + 3x$,　(b) $a - 3b + 2a - b$,　(c) $3 \times m \times m$.

17 Here is a formula for working out the perimeter of a rectangle $P = 2(l + w)$.
Use the formula to work out the value of P when $l = 6$ and $w = 4$.
Edexcel

18 (a) Find the value of $\dfrac{3(m + 9)}{n}$ when $m = -5$ and $n = 24$.
(b) Find the value of $3p + q$ when $p = -2$ and $q = 5$.

19 Solve　(a) $x + 7 = 4$,　(b) $4x = 10$,　(c) $\dfrac{x}{2} = 3$,　(d) $2x + 5 = 11$.

20 (a) Copy and complete this table of values for $y = 3x - 1$.

x	-3	-2	-1	0	1	2	3
y	-10		-4			5	

(b) Draw the graph of $y = 3x - 1$.
(c) Use your graph to find the value of x when $y = 6.5$
Edexcel

21 Find the value of $3x + y^3$ when $x = -1$ and $y = -2$.

22 (a) Simplify (i) $5c + 2c - 3c$,　(ii) $5p - 8r + 12r - 6p$.
(b) Find the value of (i) $5x + 2y$ when $x = 3$ and $y = 6$,
　　　　　　　　　　(ii) $4g - 2h$ when $g = 2$ and $h = -4$.
Edexcel

23 A sequence begins　1, -1, …　This rule is used to continue the sequence.

　　Multiply the last number by 2 and then subtract 3.

(a) What is the next term in the sequence?
(b) A term in the sequence is called x. Write, in terms of x, the next term in the sequence.

24 Multiply out　$5(3x - 2)$.
Edexcel

25 Choc Bars cost 27 pence each. Write down a formula for the cost, C pence, of n Choc Bars.
Edexcel

26 Hannah is x years old.
(a) Her sister Louisa is 3 years younger than Hannah.
　　Write an expression, in terms of x, for Louisa's age.
(b) Their mother is four times as old as Hannah.
　　Write an expression, in terms of x, for their mother's age.
(c) The total of their ages is 45 years.
　　By forming an equation in x, find their ages.

27 Factorise　$9x + 12$.
Edexcel

28 (a) Factorise　$k^2 - 2k$.
(b) Solve (i) $3 - 4x = x + 8$,　(ii) $3(2x + 1) = 6$.

29 Given that $s = 2t^3$, find the value of t when $s = 250$.

30 $y = \frac{4}{5}(9 - x)$. Find the value of x when $y = 6$.

31 Solve the equation $\frac{3x - 5}{8} = 5$. *Edexcel*

32 $-2 < x \leq 1$. x is an integer. Write down all the possible values of x. *Edexcel*

33 (a) On the same diagram draw the graphs $2y = x + 4$ and $y = \frac{1}{2}x + 1$.
(b) What do you notice about the two lines you have drawn?

34 The fraction, p, of an adult's dose of medicine which should be given to a child who weighs w kg is given by the formula $p = \frac{3w + 20}{200}$.
A child weighs 35 kg.
(a) Work out the fraction of an adult's dose which should be given to this child.
Give your answer as a fraction in its simplest form.
(b) Use the formula $p = \frac{3w + 20}{200}$ to find the weight of a child whose dose is the same as an adult's dose. *Edexcel*

35 Here are the first five numbers of a simple number sequence. 1, 5, 9, 13, 17, ...
(a) Write down the next two numbers in the sequence.
(b) Describe, in words, the rule to continue this sequence.
(c) Write down, in terms of n, the nth term in this sequence. *Edexcel*

36 (a) Solve the inequality $3x < 8 - x$ and show the solution on a number line.
(b) List all the values of n, where n is an integer, such that $-3 < 2n + 1 \leq 3$.

37 Match these equations to their graphs.

A $y = x$
B $y + x = 1$
C $y = x^2$
D $y = x^3$

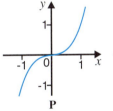
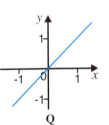
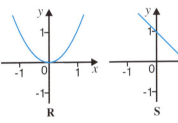

P   Q   R   S

38 Simplify. (a) $\frac{p^6}{p^2}$ (b) $q^3 \times q$ *Edexcel*

39 (a) A sequence begins: -2, 1, 4, 7, 10, ...
Write, in terms of n, the nth term of the sequence.
(b) Make x the subject of the formula $y = 2x - 5$.

40 (a) Copy and complete the table of values for $y = x^2 - 2x + 1$.

x	-1	0	1	2	3
y		1	0		4

(b) Draw the graph of $y = x^2 - 2x + 1$ for values of x from -1 to 3.
(c) Use your graph to solve the equations (i) $x^2 - 2x + 1 = 0$, (ii) $x^2 - 2x + 1 = 2$.

41 Water is poured into a container at a constant rate.
Copy the axes given and sketch the graph of the depth of the water against time as the container is filled.

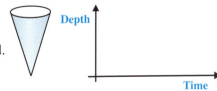

42 (a) Multiply out and simplify $(p - 2)(p + 2)$.
(b) Simplify $\frac{q^3 \times q^5}{q^2}$.

43 Expand and simplify $3(2x - 1) - 2(2x - 3)$. *Edexcel*

Algebra Calculator Paper

You may use a calculator for this exercise.

1 (a) A sequence begins: 1, 2, 4, 7, 11, 16, ...
  (i) What is the next term in the sequence?
  (ii) Describe the rule you used to find the next term.
 (b) Another sequence uses this rule:

  > Add 3 to the last term.

  What term comes before 15 in this sequence?

2 (a) Simplify. (i) $y + 2y + 3y$ (ii) $3m + 4 + m - 3$
 (b) Work out the missing values in these calculations.
  (i) $10 \rightarrow \boxed{-3} \rightarrow \boxed{\times 2} \rightarrow \ldots$ (ii) $\ldots \rightarrow \boxed{-3} \rightarrow \boxed{\times 2} \rightarrow 10$

3 (a) A ball costs x pence. How much will 3 balls cost?
 (b) A skipping rope costs 30 pence more than a ball. How much does a skipping rope cost?

4 Cheryl was working out the cost of hiring a van for a day.
 First of all she worked out the mileage cost. She used the formula:

 > Mileage cost = Mileage rate × Number of miles travelled

 The mileage rate was 9 pence per mile. Cheryl travelled 240 miles.
 (a) Work out the mileage cost.

 Cheryl worked out the total hire cost by using the formula:

 > Total hire cost = Basic hire cost + Mileage cost

 The basic hire cost was £45.
 (b) Work out the total hire cost.

 Edexcel

5 (a) Pablo has £t. He spends £3. How much has he got left?
 (b) Cynthia has x five pound notes and $2x$ ten pound notes.
  Write an expression, in terms of x, for the total value of her notes.

6 Here are the first five numbers in a simple number sequence.
  1, 3, 7, 13, 21, ...
 (a) Write down the next two numbers in the sequence.
 (b) Describe, in words, the rule to continue this sequence.

 Edexcel

7 This conversion graph can be used to change euros to dollars.

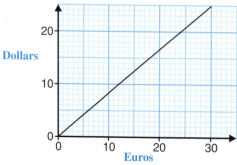

 (a) Use the graph to find (i) 30 euros in dollars, (ii) 15 dollars in euros.
 (b) Explain how you can use the graph to change 100 dollars into euros.

8 Maureen thought of a number. She divided this number by 4. She then added 3.
Her answer was 9.
What number did Maureen think of? *Edexcel*

9 Powder can be mixed with water to make a milk drink.

This rule is used: | Number of spoonfuls = Amount of water (ml) ÷ 30 |

A glass contains 180 ml of water.
(a) How many spoonfuls are needed?

There are 20 spoonfuls of powder in a jug.
(b) How much water is needed? *Edexcel*

10 Solve these equations. (a) $g - 5 = 3$ (b) $4 + a = 9$ (c) $7x = 42$ (d) $5x + 4 = 19$

11 Umbrellas cost £4 each.
(a) Write a formula for the cost, C, in pounds, of u umbrellas.
(b) Find the value of u when $C = 28$.

12 (a) Find the value of $3m - 5$ when $m = 4$.
(b) $T = 3m - 5$. Find the value of m when $T = 4$.
(c) $P = 5y^2$. Find the value of P when $y = 3$.

13 Here is a formula for working out a printing cost.

printing cost = price per sheet of paper × number of sheets of paper + fixed charge

The price per sheet of paper is £0.04. 2500 sheets of paper are used.
The fixed charge is £45.50.
Work out the printing cost. *Edexcel*

14 (a) Simplify (i) $x + x + x$ (ii) $2a + 4b + a - 2b$ (iii) $3(a + 2)$
(b) Expand and simplify $2(x - 1) + 3(2x + 1)$ *Edexcel*

15 The graph shows the journey of a cyclist from Cordy to Dalton and back.

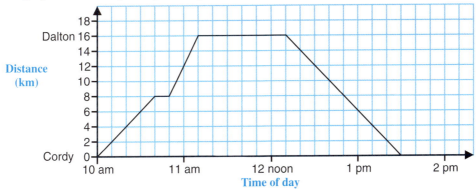

(a) On the way to Dalton, the cyclist stopped for a rest.
For how long did the cyclist stop?
(b) During which part of the journey did the cyclist travel the fastest? Explain your answer.
(c) What was the average speed of the cyclist from Dalton back to Cordy?

16 (a) Solve $4p + 6 = 26$.
(b) Solve $5(2q + 6) = 25$.
(c) Solve $18y - 27 = 10y - 25$. *Edexcel*

17 (a) Draw the line $y = 2x + 1$ for values of x from -1 to 2.
(b) The line $y = 2x + 1$ crosses the line $x = -5$ at P. Give the coordinates of P.

18 Here is a rule to change kilograms to pounds.

> Multiply the number of kilograms by 22 and then divide by 10.

(a) Use the rule to change 5 kilograms to pounds.
(b) Write a formula to change K kilograms to L pounds.
(c) Use your formula to find the value of K when $L = 55$.

19 (a) Expand. $t(t - 2)$
(b) Factorise. $3y - 12$
Edexcel

20 (a) Solve the equations (i) $4(a - 2) = 6$, (ii) $5t + 3 = -1 + t$.
(b) The sum of the numbers x, $x - 3$ and $x + 7$ is 25.
By forming an equation in x, find the value of x.

21 The equation $x^3 - 15x = 31$ has a solution between 4 and 5.
Use a trial and improvement method to find this solution.
Give your answer correct to one decimal place.
You must show **ALL** your working.
Edexcel

22 (a) Simplify (i) $x^6 \div x^2$ (ii) $y^4 \times y^4$.
(b) Expand and simplify $(t + 4)(t - 2)$.
(c) Write down the integer values of x that satisfy the inequality $-2 \leqslant x < 4$.
Edexcel

23 (a) Here are the first four terms of a simple sequence.

$$5, \quad 11, \quad 17, \quad 23$$

Write, in terms of n, the nth term of the sequence.
(b) The nth term of another sequence is $n^2 + 3$.
Write down the first and second terms of the sequence.

24 A shop sells Big lollipops at 80p each and Small lollipops at 60p each.
Henry buys x Big lollipops.
(a) Write down an expression, in terms of x, for the cost of Henry's lollipops.

Lucy buys r Big lollipops and t Small lollipops.
(b) Write down an expression, in terms of r and t, for the total cost of Lucy's lollipops.

The cost of g Big lollipops and 2 Small lollipops is £10.80.
(c) (i) Write this as an equation in terms of g.
(ii) Use your equation to find the value of g.
Edexcel

25 (a) Copy and complete the table of values for $y = x^2 - 5$.

x	−3	−2	−1	0	1	2	3
y	4		−4	−5			4

(b) Draw the graph of $y = x^2 - 5$ for values of x from -3 to 3.
(c) Use your graph to solve the equation $x^2 - 5 = 0$.

26 The equation $x^3 + 4x = 100$ has one solution which is a positive number.
Use the method of trial and improvement to find this solution.
Give your answer correct to 1 decimal place.
You must show **ALL** working.
Edexcel

27 (a) Solve the equation $3 - x = 4(x + 1)$.
(b) Multiply out and simplify $2(5x - 3) - 3(x - 1)$.
(c) Simplify (i) $m^8 \div m^2$, (ii) $n^2 \times n^3$.

28 (a) List all the values of n, where n is an integer, such that $-3 \leqslant n - 1 < 1$.
(b) Factorise $m^2 + mn$.

SECTION 21 — Angles

What you need to know

- You should be able to use a **protractor** to measure and draw angles accurately.

  Eg 1 Measure the size of this angle.

  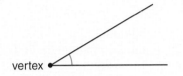

  vertex

  The angle measures 30°.

  To measure an angle, the protractor is placed so that its centre point is on the corner (vertex) of the angle, with the base along one of the arms of the angle, as shown.

- Types and names of angles.

Acute angle	Right angle	Obtuse angle	Reflex angle
$0° < a < 90°$	$a = 90°$	$90° < a < 180°$	$180° < a < 360°$

- Angle properties.

Angles at a point	Complementary angles	Supplementary angles	Vertically opposite angles
			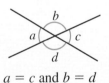
$a + b + c = 360°$	$x + y = 90°$	$a + b = 180°$	$a = c$ and $b = d$

- A straight line joining two points is called a **line segment**.
- Lines which meet at right angles are **perpendicular** to each other.
- Lines which never meet and are always the same distance apart are **parallel**.
- When two parallel lines are crossed by a **transversal** the following pairs of angles are formed.

Corresponding angles	Alternate angles	Allied angles
$a = c$	$b = c$	$b + d = 180°$

  Arrowheads are used to show that lines are **parallel**.

- You should be able to use angle properties to solve problems involving lines and angles.

  Eg 2 Work out the size of the angles marked with letters.
  Give a reason for each answer.

  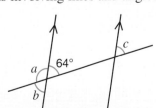

  $a + 64° = 180°$ (supplementary angles)
  $a = 180° - 64° = 116°$

  $b = 64°$ (vertically opposite angles)
  $c = 64°$ (corresponding angles)

Exercise 21

1 Look at the diagram.

(a) Which lines are parallel to each other?
(b) Which lines are perpendicular to each other?
(c) (i) Measure angle *y*.
 (ii) Which of these words describes angle *y*?

acute angle   obtuse angle   reflex angle

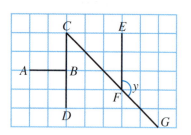

2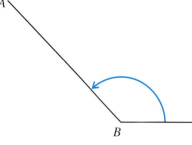

(a) Measure the size of angle *ABC*.

(b) Copy the diagram.
 D is the point such that angle *BCD* is 102°
 and angle *BAD* is 68°.
 Mark the position of *D* on your diagram.

Edexcel

3 Find the size of the lettered angles. Give a reason for each answer.

(a)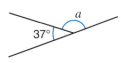

(b)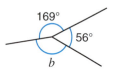

(c)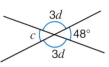

4 (a) (i) Work out the size of angle *p*.
 (ii) Give a reason for your answer.

(b) (i) Work out the size of angle *q*.
 (ii) Give a reason for your answer.

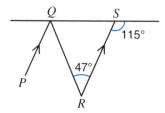

Edexcel

5 In the diagram, the lines *PQ* and *RS* are parallel.

(a) What is the size of angle *PQR*?
 Give a reason for your answer.

(b) Find the size of angle *RQS*.

6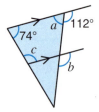

Work out the size of the angles marked with letters.
Give a reason for each answer.

7 Find the size of the angles marked with letters.

(a)

(b)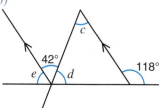

(c)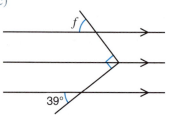

SECTION 22 — Triangles

What you need to know

- Triangles can be: **acute-angled** (all angles less than 90°),
  obtuse-angled (one angle greater than 90°),
  right-angled (one angle equal to 90°).

- The sum of the angles in a triangle is 180°.
  $a + b + c = 180°$

- The exterior angle is equal to the sum of the two opposite interior angles. $a + b = d$

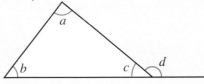

- Types of triangle:

  Scalene — Sides have different lengths. Angles are all different.

  Isosceles — Two equal sides. Two equal angles.

  Equilateral — Three equal sides. Three equal angles, 60°.

  A **sketch** is used when an accurate drawing is not required. Dashes across lines show sides that are equal in length. Equal angles are marked using arcs.

- You should be able to use properties of triangles to solve problems.

  Eg 1 Find the size of the angles marked a and b.

  $a = 86° + 51°$ (ext. ∠ of a ∆)
  $a = 137°$
  $b + 137° = 180°$ (supp. ∠'s)
  $b = 43°$

  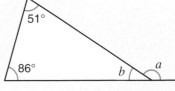

- Perimeter of a triangle is the sum of its three sides.

- Area of a triangle = $\dfrac{\text{base} \times \text{perpendicular height}}{2}$

  $A = \tfrac{1}{2} \times b \times h$

   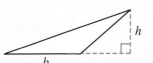

  Eg 2 Calculate the area of this triangle.

  $A = \tfrac{1}{2} \times b \times h$
  $= \tfrac{1}{2} \times 9 \times 6 \text{ cm}^2$
  $= 27 \text{ cm}^2$

- You should be able to draw triangles accurately, using ruler, compasses and protractor.

Exercise 22

1 Without measuring, work out the size of the angles marked with letters.

(a)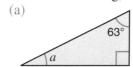

(b)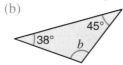

(c)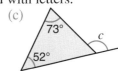

2 ABC and EBD are straight lines.
BD = BC. Angle CBD = 42°.

(a) Write down the size of the angle marked $e°$.

(b) Work out the size of the angle marked $f°$.

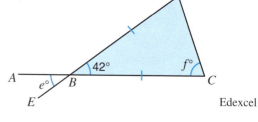

Edexcel

3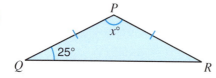

The diagram shows triangle PQR, with PQ = PR.
Work out the value of x.
Give a reason for your answer.

4 (a) (i) Write down the size of the angle marked $x°$.
(ii) Give a reason for your answer.

(b) (i) Work out the size of the angle marked $y°$.
(ii) Give a reason for your answer.

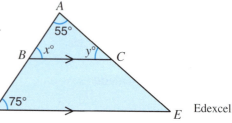

Edexcel

5 The diagram shows an isosceles triangle with two sides extended.

(a) Work out the size of angle x.

(b) Work out the size of angle y.

6 Make accurate drawings of these triangles using the information given.
(a)   (b)   (c)

7 Find the areas of these triangles.
(a)   (b)   (c)

8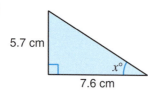

The diagram shows a sketch of a triangle.
(a) Make an accurate drawing of the triangle.
(b) (i) On your drawing, measure the size of the angle marked $x°$.
(ii) What is the special mathematical name of the angle marked $x°$?
(c) Work out the area of the triangle.

Edexcel

9 The diagram shows triangle ABC.
Calculate the area of triangle ABC.

SECTION  **Symmetry and Congruence**

What you need to know

- A two-dimensional shape has **line symmetry** if the line divides the shape so that one side fits exactly over the other.

- A two-dimensional shape has **rotational symmetry** if it fits into a copy of its outline as it is rotated through 360°.

- A shape is only described as having rotational symmetry if the order of rotational symmetry is 2 or more.

- The number of times a shape fits into its outline in a single turn is the **order of rotational symmetry**.

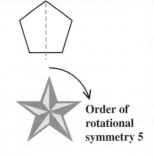

Order of rotational symmetry 5

Eg 1 For each of these shapes (a) draw and state the number of lines of symmetry,
(b) state the order of rotational symmetry.

(i) 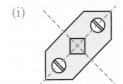   (ii) 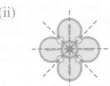   (iii)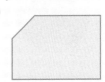

Two lines of symmetry. Rotational symmetry of order 2.

4 lines of symmetry. Order of rotational symmetry 4.

No lines of symmetry. Order of rotational symmetry 1. The shape is **not** described as having rotational symmetry.

- A **plane of symmetry** slices through a three-dimensional object so that one half is the mirror image of the other half.

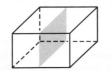

- Three-dimensional objects can have **axes of symmetry**.

Eg 2 Sketch a cuboid and show its axes of symmetry.

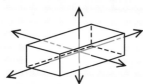

A cuboid has three axes of symmetry. The order of rotational symmetry about each axis is 2.

- When two shapes are the same shape and size they are said to be **congruent**.

- There are four ways to show that a pair of triangles are congruent.

SSS 3 corresponding sides.	**ASA** 2 angles and a corresponding side.
SAS 2 sides and the included angle.	**RHS** Right angle, hypotenuse and one other side.

Eg 3 Which of these triangles are congruent to each other? Give a reason for your answer.

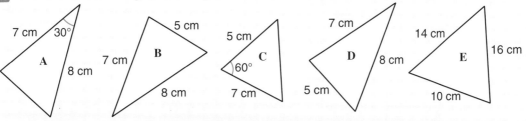

B and D.   Reason: 3 corresponding sides (SSS)

Exercise 23

1 Copy and reflect each of the shapes in the mirror lines given.

(a) (b)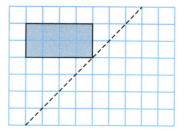

Edexcel

2 Consider the letters of the word **O R A N G E**

Which letters have (a) line symmetry only,
(b) rotational symmetry only,
(c) line symmetry and rotational symmetry?

3 For each of these shapes state (i) the number of lines of symmetry,
(ii) the order of rotational symmetry.

(a) 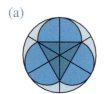 (b) (c) (d)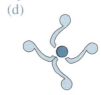

4 The diagram shows a square grid with two squares shaded.
Copy the diagram and shade two more squares so that the final diagram has rotational symmetry of order 2.

5 The diagram represents a prism.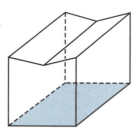

Copy the diagram and draw in one plane of symmetry on your diagram.

Edexcel

6 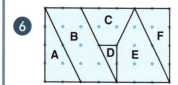 The diagram shows a rectangle which has been cut into 6 pieces.
Which two pieces are congruent to each other?

7 The diagram shows information about four triangles.
Which two triangles are congruent?
Give a reason for your answer.

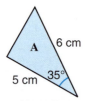 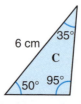 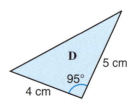

58

SECTION 24 — Quadrilaterals

What you need to know

- A **quadrilateral** is a shape made by four straight lines.
- The sum of the angles in a quadrilateral is 360°.
- The **perimeter** of a quadrilateral is the sum of the lengths of its four sides.
- Facts about these special quadrilaterals:

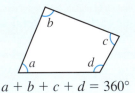

$a + b + c + d = 360°$

rectangle   square   parallelogram   rhombus   trapezium   isosceles trapezium   kite

Quadrilateral	Sides	Angles	Diagonals	Line symmetry	Order of rotational symmetry	Area formula
Rectangle	Opposite sides equal and parallel	All 90°	Bisect each other	2	2	$A =$ length $\times$ breadth $A = lb$
Square	4 equal sides, opposite sides parallel	All 90°	Bisect each other at 90°	4	4	$A = $ (length)^2 $A = l^2$
Parallelogram	Opposite sides equal and parallel	Opposite angles equal	Bisect each other	0	2	$A = $ base $\times$ height $A = bh$
Rhombus	4 equal sides, opposite sides parallel	Opposite angles equal	Bisect each other at 90°	2	2	$A = $ base $\times$ height $A = bh$
Trapezium	1 pair of parallel sides					$A = \frac{1}{2}(a+b)h$
Isosceles trapezium	1 pair of parallel sides, non-parallel sides equal	2 pairs of equal angles	Equal in length	1	1*	$A = \frac{1}{2}(a+b)h$
Kite	2 pairs of adjacent sides equal	1 pair of opposite angles equal	One bisects the other at 90°	1	1*	

*A shape is only described as having rotational symmetry if the order of rotational symmetry is 2 or more.

- You should be able to use properties of quadrilaterals to solve problems.

  Eg 1 Work out the size of the angle marked x.

  Opposite angles are equal.
  So, $125° + 125° + x + x = 360°$
  $x = 55°$

  Eg 2 Find the area of this trapezium.

  $A = \frac{1}{2}(a+b)h$
  $= \frac{1}{2}(6+9)5$
  $= \frac{1}{2} \times 15 \times 5$
  $= 37.5 \text{ cm}^2$

- You should be able to construct a quadrilateral from given information using ruler, protractor, compasses.

Exercise 24

1 This rectangle is drawn on 1 cm squared paper.
It has a perimeter of 18 cm.
(a) What is the area of the rectangle?
(b) (i) On 1 cm squared paper draw three different rectangles which each have a perimeter of 18 cm.
(ii) Find the area of each rectangle.

Not full size

2 (a) Name each quadrilateral which has all its sides of equal length.
(b) Name each quadrilateral which has only one pair of parallel sides.
(c) Name each quadrilateral which has two pairs of parallel sides, but no angles of 90° between its sides.

Edexcel

3 Find the size of the lettered angles.
(a)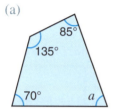
(b)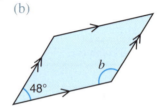
(c)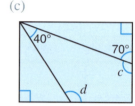

4 (a) (i) Work out the value of x.
(ii) Give a reason for your answer.
(b) (i) Work out the value of y.
(ii) Give a reason for your answer.

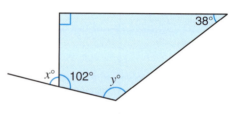

Edexcel

5 The diagram shows a quadrilateral ABCD.
$AB = BC$ and $CD = DA$.
(a) Which of the following correctly describes the quadrilateral ABCD?
rhombus   parallelogram   kite   trapezium
(b) Angle $ADC = 36°$ and angle $BCD = 105°$.
Work out the size of angle ABC.

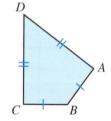

6 ABCD is a quadrilateral.
$AB = 6$ cm, $AC = 9$ cm, $BC = 5$ cm, $AD = 3.5$ cm and angle $BAD = 66°$.
Make an accurate drawing of the quadrilateral ABCD.

Edexcel

7 A rectangle measures 8.6 cm by 6.4 cm.
(a) Find the perimeter of the rectangle.
(b) Find the area of the rectangle.

8 The perimeter of this rectangle is 22 cm.
The length of the rectangle is 8 cm.
Work out the area of the rectangle.

Edexcel

9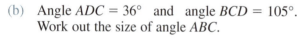

The diagram shows a trapezium PQRS.
(a) Work out the size of the angle marked x.
(b) Calculate the area of the trapezium.

SECTION 25 Polygons

What you need to know

- A **polygon** is a many-sided shape made by straight lines.
- A polygon with all sides equal and all angles equal is called a **regular polygon**.
- Shapes you need to know:
  A 3-sided polygon is called a **triangle**.
  A 4-sided polygon is called a **quadrilateral**.
  A 5-sided polygon is called a **pentagon**.
  A 6-sided polygon is called a **hexagon**.
  An 8-sided polygon is called an **octagon**.
- The sum of the exterior angles of any polygon is 360°.
- At each vertex of a polygon: interior angle + exterior angle = 180°
- The sum of the interior angles of an *n*-sided polygon is given by:
  $(n - 2) \times 180°$
- For a regular *n*-sided polygon: exterior angle = $\frac{360°}{n}$
- You should be able to use the properties of polygons to solve problems.

Eg 1 Find the sum of the interior angles of a pentagon.
$(5 - 2) \times 180° = 3 \times 180° = 540°$

A pentagon has 5 sides, so, substitute $n = 5$ into $(n - 2) \times 180°$.

Eg 2 A regular polygon has an exterior angle of 30°.
(a) How many sides has the polygon?
(b) What is the size of an interior angle of the polygon?

(a) $n = \frac{360°}{\text{exterior angle}}$
$n = \frac{360°}{30°}$
$n = 12$

(b) int. ∠ + ext. ∠ = 180°
int. ∠ + 30° = 180°
interior angle = 150°

- A shape will **tessellate** if it covers a surface without overlapping and leaves no gaps.
- All triangles tessellate.
- All quadrilaterals tessellate.
- Equilateral triangles, squares and hexagons can be used to make **regular tessellations**.

Exercise 25

1 These shapes are drawn on isometric paper.

What are the differences between the symmetry of shape *A* and the symmetry of shape *B*?

2 Work out the size of the angles marked with letters.

(a)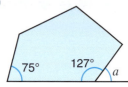
(b)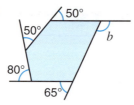
(c)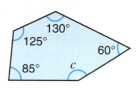

3 These shapes are regular polygons. Work out the size of the lettered angles.

(a)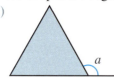
(b)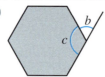
(c)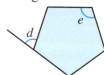

4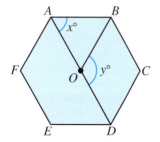

ABCDEF is a regular hexagon with centre O.
(a) What type of triangle is ABO?
(b) (i) Work out the size of the angle marked $x°$.
    (ii) Work out the size of the angle marked $y°$.
(c) (i) What type of quadrilateral is BCDO?
    (ii) Draw a diagram to show how three such quadrilaterals can tessellate to make a hexagon.

Edexcel

5 (a) Here is a pattern of regular octagons and squares. Explain why these shapes tessellate.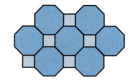

(b) Draw a tessellation which uses equilateral triangles and regular hexagons.

6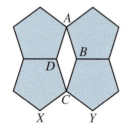

Four regular pentagons are placed together, as shown, to form a rhombus, ABCD.

Calculate the size of
(a) angle ABC,
(b) angle XCY.

7 The diagram shows part of a regular polygon. The exterior angles of this polygon are 24°. How many sides has the polygon?

8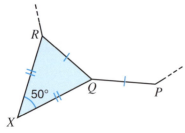

PQ and QR are two sides of a regular 10-sided polygon.
QRX is an isosceles triangle with RX = XQ.
Angle QXR = 50°.

Work out the size of the obtuse angle PQX.

9 The diagram shows part of an inscribed regular polygon. The line AB is one side of the polygon.
O is the centre of the circle.
Angle AOB = 30°.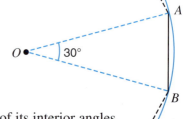

Show that the polygon has 12 sides and hence find the sum of its interior angles.

SECTION 26 — Direction and Distance

What you need to know

- **Compass points**

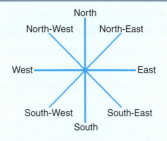

  The angle between North and East is 90°.
  The angle between North and North-East is 45°.

- **Bearings** are used to describe the direction in which you must travel to get from one place to another.

- A bearing is an angle measured from the North line in a clockwise direction.
  A bearing can be any angle from 0° to 360° and is written as a three-figure number.

  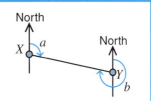

  To find a bearing:
  measure angle a to find the bearing of Y from X,
  measure angle b to find the bearing of X from Y.

- You should be able to use **scales** and **bearings** to interpret and draw accurate diagrams.

  There are two ways to describe a scale.
  1. A scale of 1 cm to 10 km means that a distance of 1 cm on the map represents an actual distance of 10 km.
  2. A scale of 1 : 10 000 means that all distances measured on the map have to be multiplied by 10 000 to find the real distance.

Eg 1 The diagram shows the plan of a stage in a car rally.
The plan has been drawn to a scale of 1 : 50 000.

(a) What is the bearing of Q from P?
(b) What is the bearing of P from R?
(c) What is the actual distance from P to R in metres?

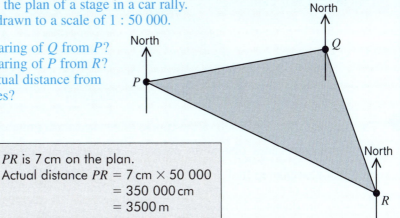

(a) 080°
(b) 295°
(c) 3500 m

PR is 7 cm on the plan.
Actual distance PR = 7 cm × 50 000
= 350 000 cm
= 3500 m

Exercise 26

1 Jon is facing North-West.
He turns through 180°.
In which direction is he now facing?

2 Here is a plan of a town.
Some buildings are shown on it.

Write down the compass bearing of
(a) the Office block from the Castle,
(b) the Windmill from the Office block,
(c) the Church from the Castle.

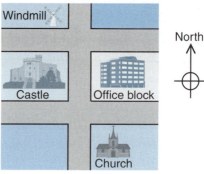

Edexcel

3 A bridge is 2600 m in length.
A plan of the bridge has been drawn to a scale of 1 cm to 100 m.
What is the length of the bridge on the plan?

4 The dot represents a Lighthouse.
The cross represents a Ship.

Measure the 3-figure bearing
of the Ship from the Lighthouse.

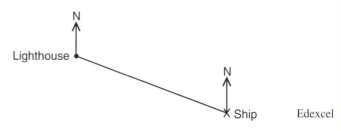

Edexcel

5 The map shows the positions of a windmill, W, and a pylon, P.
(a) What is the bearing of
(i) the pylon from the windmill,
(ii) the windmill from the pylon?

The map has been drawn to a scale of 2 cm to 5 km.
(b) Use the map to find the distance WP in kilometres.

6 The map shows part of a coastline and a Coastguard Station.
1 cm on the map represents 2 km.
A ship is 12 km from the Coastguard Station on a bearing of 160°.
Copy the map and plot the position of the ship from the Coastguard Station, using a scale of 1 cm to represent 2 km.

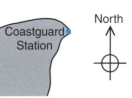

Edexcel

7 The diagram shows a sketch of the course to be used for a running event.

(a) Draw an accurate plan of the course, using a scale of 1 cm to represent 100 m.

(b) Use your plan to find
(i) the bearing of X from Y,
(ii) the distance XY in metres.

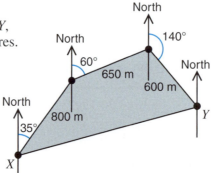

SECTION 27 — Circles

What you need to know

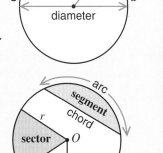

- A **circle** is the shape drawn by keeping a pencil the same distance from a fixed point on a piece of paper.
- Words associated with circles:

  Circumference – perimeter of a circle.

  Radius – distance from the centre of the circle to any point on the circumference. The plural of radius is **radii**.

  Diameter – distance right across the circle, passing through the centre point.

  Chord – a line joining two points on the circumference.

  Tangent – a line which touches the circumference of a circle at one point only. A tangent is perpendicular to the radius at the point of contact.

  Arc – part of the circumference of a circle.

  Segment – a chord divides a circle into two segments.

  Sector – two radii divide a circle into two sectors.

- The **circumference** of a circle is given by: $C = \pi \times d$ or $C = 2 \times \pi \times r$
- The **area** of a circle is given by: $A = \pi \times r^2$
- You should be able to solve problems which involve finding the circumference or the area of a circle.
- Take π to be 3.14 or use the π key on your calculator.

Eg 1 Calculate the circumference of a circle with diameter 18 cm.
Give your answer to 1 d.p.
$C = \pi \times d$
$C = \pi \times 18$
$C = 56.548...$ $\qquad C = 56.5$ cm, correct to 1 d.p.

Eg 2 Find the area of a circle with radius 6 cm.
Give your answer to 3 sig. figs.
$A = \pi \times r^2$
$A = \pi \times 6 \times 6$
$A = 113.097...$ $\qquad A = 113$ cm², correct to 3 sig. figs.

Eg 3 A circle has a circumference of 25.2 cm.
Find the diameter of the circle.
$C = \pi d$ so, $d = \dfrac{C}{\pi}$
$d = \dfrac{25.2}{\pi}$
$d = 8.021...$ $\qquad d = 8.0$ cm, correct to 1 d.p.

Eg 4 A circle has an area of 154 cm².
Find the radius of the circle.
$A = \pi r^2$ so, $r^2 = \dfrac{A}{\pi}$
$r^2 = \dfrac{154}{\pi} = 49.019...$
$r = \sqrt{49.019...} = 7.001...$ $\qquad r = 7$ cm, to the nearest cm.

Exercise 27

Do not use a calculator for question 1.

1 A circular pond has a diameter of 9.8 metres.
  (a) Estimate the circumference of the pond.
  (b) Estimate the area of the pond.

2 A circle has a diameter of 5 cm.
  (a) Calculate the circumference of the circle.
  (b) Calculate the area of the circle.
  Give your answers correct to one decimal place.

3 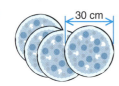 Discs of card are used in the packaging of frozen pizzas.
  Each disc fits the base of the pizza exactly.
  Calculate the area of a disc used to pack a pizza.
  Give your answer in terms of π.

4 A circle has a radius of 32 cm. Work out the circumference of the circle.
  Give your answer correct to the nearest centimetre.
  Edexcel

5 Tranter has completed three-fifths of a circular jigsaw puzzle.
  The puzzle has a radius of 20 cm.
  What area of the puzzle is complete?

6 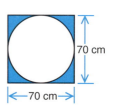 Mr Kray's lawn is 25 m in length.
  He rolls it with a garden roller.
  The garden roller has a diameter of 0.4 m.
  Work out the number of times the roller rotates when rolling the length of the lawn once.

7 The radius of a circle is 5.1 m.
  Work out the area of the circle.
  Edexcel

8 The diagram shows a circle of diameter 70 cm inside a square of side 70 cm.
  Work out the area of the shaded part of the diagram.
  Edexcel

9 Each wheel on Hannah's bicycle has a radius of 15 cm.
  Calculate how many complete revolutions each wheel makes when Hannah cycles 100 metres.

10  A table has a top in the shape of a circle with a radius of 45 centimetres.
  (a) Calculate the area of the circular table top.

  The base of the table is also in the shape of a circle.
  The circumference of this circle is 110 centimetres.
  (b) Calculate the diameter of the base of the table.
  Edexcel

11 Three circles overlap, as shown.
  The largest circle has a diameter of 12 cm.
  The ratio of the diameters $x : y$ is $1 : 2$.
  Calculate the shaded area.
  Give your answer in terms of π.

12 A circle has a circumference of 100 cm.
  Calculate the area of the circle. Give your answer correct to three significant figures.

13 Alfie says, *"A semi-circle with a radius of 10 cm has a larger area than a whole circle with half the radius."* Is he correct?
  You **must** show working to justify your answer.

SECTION 28

Areas and Volumes

What you need to know

- Shapes formed by joining different shapes together are called **compound shapes**.
  To find the area of a compound shape we must first divide the shape up into rectangles, triangles, circles, etc., and find the area of each part.
  Add the answers to find the total area.

  Eg 1 Find the total area of this shape.

  Area $A = 5 \times 4 = 20\,cm^2$
  Area $B = 6 \times 3 = 18\,cm^2$
  Total area $= 20 + 18 = 38\,cm^2$

  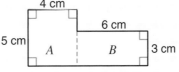

- **Faces**, **vertices** (corners) and **edges**.

  Eg 2 A cube has 6 faces, 8 vertices and 12 edges.

  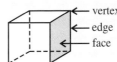

- A **net** can be used to make a solid shape.

  Eg 3 Draw a net of a cube.

- **Isometric paper** is used to make 2-D drawings of 3-D shapes.

  Eg 4 Draw a cube of edge 2 cm on isometric paper.

- **Plans and Elevations**
  The view of a 3-D shape looking from above is called a **plan**.
  The view of a 3-D shape from the front or sides is called an **elevation**.

  Eg 5 Draw diagrams to show the plan and elevation from **X**, for this 3-dimensional shape.

  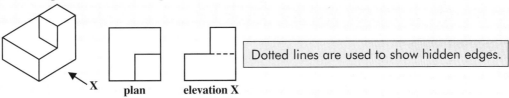

  Dotted lines are used to show hidden edges.

- **Volume** is the amount of space occupied by a 3-dimensional shape.

- The formula for the volume of a **cuboid** is:
  Volume = length × breadth × height
  $V = l \times b \times h$

- Volume of a **cube** is: $V = l^3$

  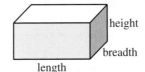

- To find the **surface area** of a cuboid, find the areas of the 6 rectangular faces and add the answers together.

  Eg 6 Find the volume and surface area of a cuboid measuring 7 cm by 5 cm by 3 cm.

  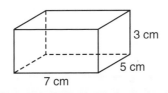

  Volume $= l \times b \times h$
  $= 7\,cm \times 5\,cm \times 3\,cm$
  $= 105\,cm^3$
  Surface area $= (2 \times 7 \times 5) + (2 \times 5 \times 3) + (2 \times 3 \times 7)$
  $= 70 + 30 + 42$
  $= 142\,cm^2$

Eg 7 This cuboid has a volume of 75 cm³.
Calculate the height, h, of the cuboid.
Volume = lbh
$$75 = 6 \times 5 \times h$$
$$h = \frac{75}{30}$$
$$h = 2.5 \text{ cm}$$

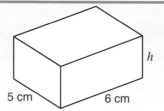

- **Prisms**
  If you make a cut at right angles to the length of a prism you will always get the same cross-section.

  Triangular prism
  cross-section
  length

- Volume of a prism = area of cross-section × length

  Eg 8 Calculate the volume of this prism.
  The cross-section of this prism is a trapezium.
  Area of cross-section = $\frac{1}{2}(5 + 3) \times 2.5$
  $$= 4 \times 2.5$$
  $$= 10 \text{ cm}^2$$
  Volume of prism = area of cross-section × length
  $$= 10 \times 12$$
  $$= 120 \text{ cm}^3$$

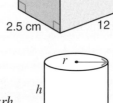

- A **cylinder** is a prism.
  Volume of a cylinder is: Volume = $\pi \times r^2 \times h$
  Surface area of a cylinder is: Surface area = $2\pi r^2 + 2\pi rh$

  Eg 9 Calculate (a) the volume,
  (b) the surface area of this cylinder.

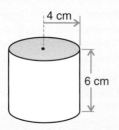

  (a) Volume = $\pi r^2 h$
  $$= \pi \times 4 \times 4 \times 6$$
  $$= 301.592\ldots$$
  $$= 302 \text{ cm}^3, \text{ correct to 3 s.f.}$$
  (b) Surface area = $2\pi r^2 + 2\pi rh$
  $$= 2 \times \pi \times 4 \times 4 + 2 \times \pi \times 4 \times 6$$
  $$= 100.53\ldots + 150.796\ldots$$
  $$= 251 \text{ cm}^2, \text{ correct to 3 s.f.}$$

Exercise 28

Do not use a calculator for question 1 to 5.

1 This shape is a pyramid.
  (a) How many faces, edges and vertices has the pyramid?
  (b) Which of these nets is a net of the pyramid?

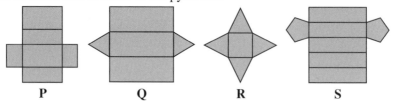

P   Q   R   S

2 The diagram shows a solid drawn on isometric paper.
  (a) Draw the plan of the solid.
  (b) Draw the elevation of the solid from the direction shown by the arrow.

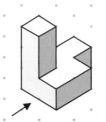

3 This shape has been drawn on 1 cm squared paper.

(a) Find the perimeter of the shape.
(b) Find the area of the shape.
(c) On 1 cm squared paper, draw a rectangle with the same perimeter.

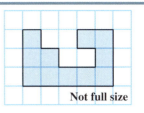
Not full size

4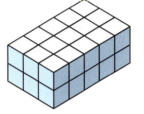

This diagram shows the floor plan of a room.
Work out the area of the floor.

Edexcel

5 This cuboid has been made using cubes of side 1 cm.

(a) How many cubes are needed to make the cuboid?
(b) (i) Draw a net of the cuboid on 1 cm squared paper.
 (ii) Hence, find the surface area of the cuboid.

6 (a) Which of these cuboids has the largest volume? Show all your working.

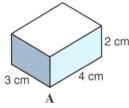 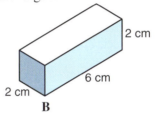 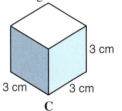
A B C

(b) (i) Draw an accurate net of cuboid **A**.
 (ii) Find the total surface area of cuboid **A**.
(c) Which cuboid has the largest surface area?

7 The diagram represents the babies' pool, with paving around, at a leisure centre.

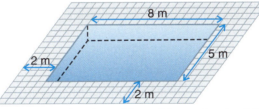

The pool is rectangular, 8 m long by 5 m wide and has a depth of 0.6 m throughout.
(a) Work out the volume of the pool in m³.

The paving around the pool is 2 m wide.
(b) Work out the area of the paving.

Edexcel

8 A mat is made in the shape of a rectangle with a semi-circle added at one end.
The width of the mat is 1.52 metres.
The length of the mat is 1.86 metres.
Calculate the area of the mat.
Give your answer in square metres, correct to 2 decimal places.

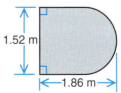

Edexcel

9 A cuboid has a volume of 100 cm³.
The cuboid is 8 cm long and 5 cm wide.
Calculate the height of the cuboid.

10 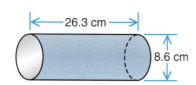 The diagram shows a cylinder.
The height of the cylinder is 26.3 cm.
The diameter of the base of the cylinder is 8.6 cm.

Calculate the volume of the cylinder.
Give your answer correct to 3 significant figures.   *Edexcel*

11 A triangular prism has dimensions, as shown.

(a) Calculate the total surface area of the prism.

(b) Calculate the volume of the prism.

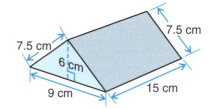

12 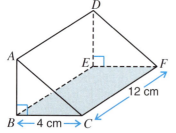 The diagram shows a triangular prism.

$BC = 4$ cm, $CF = 12$ cm and angle $ABC = 90°$.

The volume of the triangular prism is 84 cm³.
Work out the length of the side AB of the prism.   *Edexcel*

13 The diagram shows a solid object.

(a) Sketch the front elevation from the direction marked with an arrow.

(b) Sketch the plan of the solid object.

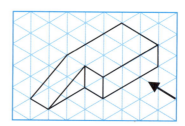

Edexcel

14 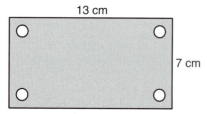 The diagram shows a rectangular metal plate with four circular holes.
The metal plate measures 13 cm by 7 cm and is 0.3 cm thick.
The radius of each circle is 0.4 cm.
Calculate the volume of the metal.

15 The diagram represents a swimming pool. The pool has vertical sides.
The pool is 8 m wide.

(a) Calculate the area of the shaded cross-section.

The swimming pool is completely filled with water.

(b) Calculate the volume of water in the pool.

64 m³ of water leaks out of the pool.

(c) Calculate the distance by which the water level falls.

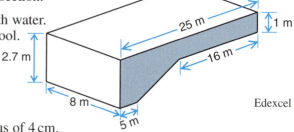

Edexcel

16 A cylinder has a height of 10 cm and a radius of 4 cm.
The cylinder is solid.
Calculate the **total** surface area of the cylinder.   *Edexcel*

17 A cylindrical water tank has radius 40 cm and height 90 cm.

(a) Calculate the total surface area of the tank.

A full tank of water is used to fill a paddling pool.

(b) The paddling pool is a square based prism, as shown.
Calculate the depth of water in the pool.

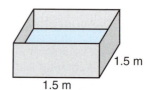

SECTION 29 — Loci and Constructions

What you need to know

- The path of a point which moves according to a rule is called a **locus**.
- The word **loci** is used when we talk about more than one locus.
- You should be able to draw the locus of a point which moves according to a given rule.

  Eg 1 A ball is rolled along this zig-zag. Draw the locus of P, the centre of the ball, as it is rolled along.

  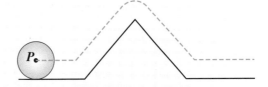

- Using a ruler and compasses you should be able to carry out the **constructions** below.

❶ The perpendicular bisector of a line.

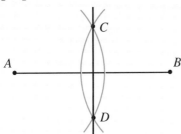

Points on the line CD are **equidistant** from the points A and B.

❷ The bisector of an angle.

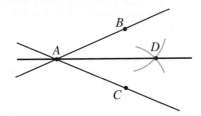

Points on the line AD are **equidistant** from the lines AB and AC.

❸ The perpendicular from a point to a line.

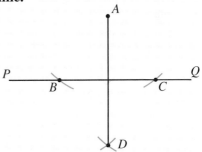

❹ The perpendicular from a point on a line.

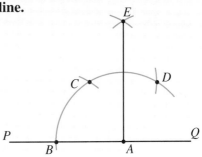

- You should be able to solve loci problems which involve using these constructions.

  Eg 2 P is a point inside triangle ABC such that:
  (i) P is equidistant from points A and B,
  (ii) P is equidistant from lines AB and BC.
  Find the position of P.

  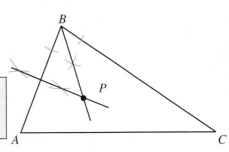

  > To find point P:
  > (i) construct the perpendicular bisector of line AB,
  > (ii) construct the bisector of angle ABC.

  P is at the point where these lines intersect.

Exercise 29

1 The ball is rolled along the zig-zag.
Copy the diagram and draw the locus of the centre of the ball as it is rolled from *X* to *Y*.

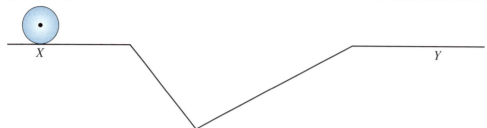

2 The diagram represents a box which is to be moved across a floor, *XY*.

Scale 1 cm to 10 cm

$AD = 30$ cm and $AB = 20$ cm.
First the box is rotated about the point *A* so that *BC* becomes vertical.
Then the box is rotated about the new position of the point *B* so that *CD* becomes vertical.
(a) Copy the diagram and make a scale drawing of the locus of the point *C*.
(b) Find the maximum height of *C* above the floor.

Edexcel

3 The map shows the positions of three villages *A*, *B* and *C*.
The map has been drawn to a scale of 1 cm to 2 km.

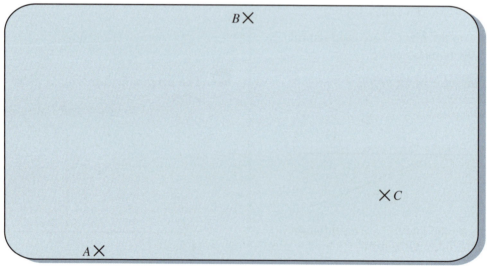

A supermarket is equidistant from villages *A*, *B* and *C*.
(a) Copy the map and find the position of the supermarket on your diagram.
(b) How many kilometres is the supermarket from village *A*?

4 (a) Construct a kite *PQRS* in which $PQ = PS = 7$ cm, $QR = RS = 5$ cm and the diagonal $QS = 6$ cm.
X is a point inside the kite such that:
(i) *X* is equidistant from *P* and *Q*,
(ii) *X* is equidistant from sides *PQ* and *PS*.
(b) By constructing the loci for (i) and (ii) find the position of *X*.
(c) Measure the distance *PX*.

SECTION 30 — Transformations

What you need to know

- The movement of a shape from one position to another is called a **transformation**.
- **Single transformations** can be described in terms of a reflection, a rotation or a translation.
- **Reflection**: The image of the shape is the same distance from the mirror line as the original.

  Eg 1 Reflect shape P in the line AB.

  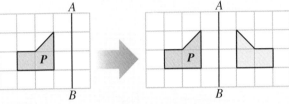

- **Rotation**: All points are turned through the same angle about the same point, called a centre of rotation.

  Eg 2 Rotate shape P 90° clockwise about the origin.

  Clockwise means:

  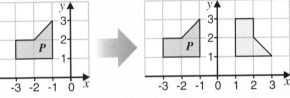

- **Translation**: All points are moved the same distance in the same direction without turning.

  Eg 3 Translate shape P with vector $\binom{3}{1}$.

  $\binom{3}{1}$ means 3 units right and 1 unit up.

  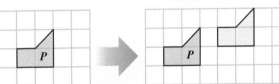

- You should be able to fully describe transformations.

Transformation	Image same shape and size?	Details needed to describe the transformation
Reflection	Yes	Mirror line, sometimes given as an equation.
Rotation	Yes	Centre of rotation, amount of turn, direction of turn.
Translation	Yes	Horizontal movement and vertical movement. Vector: top number = horizontal movement, bottom number = vertical movement.

Eg 4 Describe the single transformation which maps
(a) A onto B,
(b) C onto A,
(c) A onto D.

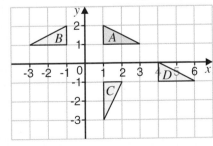

(a) **Reflection** in the y axis.
(b) **Rotation** of 90° anticlockwise about the origin.
(c) **Translation** 3 units to the right and 2 units down.

Exercise 30

1 Copy each diagram and draw the transformation given.
  (a) Reflect the shape in the *x* axis.
  (b) Translate the shape 2 units left and 3 units up.
  (c) Rotate the shape 90° clockwise about the origin.

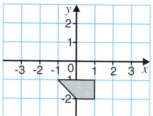
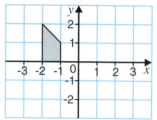

2 In each diagram *A* is mapped onto *B* by a single transformation. Describe each transformation.
  (a) (b) (c)

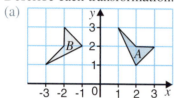
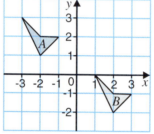
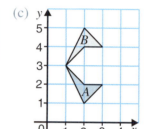

3 (a) On squared paper, draw triangle *ABC* with vertices at: *A* (1, 1), *B* (2, 3) and *C* (4, 2).
   (b) Triangle *ABC* is reflected in the *y* axis. Draw the triangle in its new position.

4 Copy the diagram.
Rotate the triangle through 90° **clockwise** about the point (0, 0).
Draw the triangle in its new position.

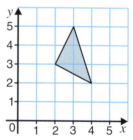

Edexcel

5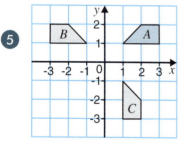

(a) Describe fully the single transformation which takes shape *A* onto shape *B*.

(b) Describe fully the single transformation which takes shape *A* onto shape *C*.

Edexcel

6 The diagram shows the positions of kites *P*, *Q* and *R*.

(a) *P* is mapped onto *Q* by a reflection. What is the equation of the line of reflection?

(b) *P* is mapped onto *R* by a translation. Describe the translation.

(c) *P* is mapped onto *T* by a rotation through 90° clockwise about (0, 3). On squared paper, copy *P* and draw the position of *T*.

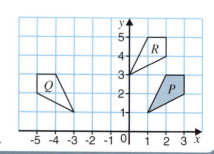

74

7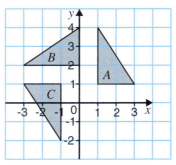

Shape A is rotated 90° anticlockwise, centre (0, 1), to shape B.
Shape B is rotated 90° anticlockwise, centre (0, 1), to shape C.
Shape C is rotated 90° anticlockwise, centre (0, 1), to shape D.

(a) Mark the position of shape D.
(b) Describe the single transformation that takes shape C to shape A.

Edexcel

8 Describe the single transformation which maps
(a) A onto B,
(b) A onto C,
(c) A onto D.

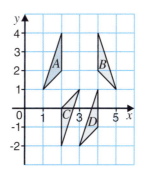

9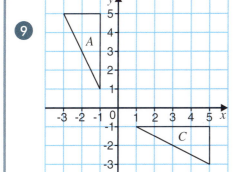

Describe fully the single transformation which maps triangle A onto triangle C.

Edexcel

10 (a) Describe fully the single transformation which maps shape P onto shape Q.

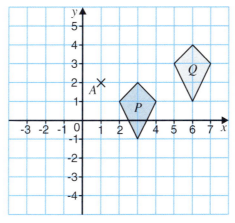

Copy shape P onto squared paper.
(b) Rotate shape P through 90° anticlockwise about the point A (1, 2).

SECTION 31 — Enlargements and Similar Figures

What you need to know

- When a shape is **enlarged**: all **lengths** are multiplied by a **scale factor**,
  angles remain unchanged.
  New length = scale factor × original length.

  The size of the original shape is:
  increased by using a scale factor greater than 1,
  reduced by using a scale factor which is a fraction, i.e. between 0 and 1.

- You should be able to draw an enlargement.

  Eg 1 Draw an enlargement of shape P, with scale factor 2, centre O.

- You should be able to describe an enlargement.

  Eg 2 Describe fully the enlargement which maps P onto Q.

  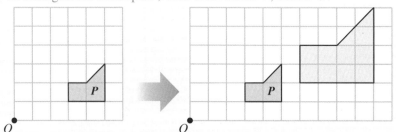

  Scale factor = $\dfrac{\text{new length}}{\text{original length}}$

  The centre of enlargement is the point where lines drawn through corresponding vertices of shapes P and Q cross.

  Enlargement, scale factor $\tfrac{1}{3}$, centre (1, 4).

- When two figures are **similar**:
  their **shapes** are the same, their **angles** are the same,
  corresponding **lengths** are in the same ratio, this ratio is the **scale factor** of the enlargement.

  Scale factor = $\dfrac{\text{new length}}{\text{original length}}$ New length = scale factor × original length

- All circles are similar to each other.

- All squares are similar to each other.

- You should be able to find corresponding lengths in similar shapes.

  Eg 3 These two shapes are similar.
  (a) Find the lengths of the sides marked x and y.
  (b) Find angle PQR.

  AB and PQ are corresponding sides.
  Scale factor = $\dfrac{PQ}{AB} = \dfrac{5}{3}$

  (a) $x = 4.5 \times \tfrac{5}{3} = 7.5\,\text{cm}$

  $y = 10 \div \tfrac{5}{3} = 6\,\text{cm}$

  (b) Angles stay the same.
  $\angle PQR = 100°$

  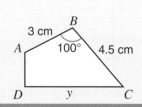
  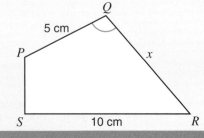

Exercise 31

1 On squared paper, enlarge ABCD by a scale factor of 2.

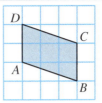

Edexcel

2 A is mapped onto B by a single transformation. Describe the transformation.

3 (a) P is mapped onto S by an enlargement. What is the centre and scale factor of the enlargement?
(b) Copy shape P onto squared paper. Draw an enlargement of shape P with scale factor 2, centre (3, 2).

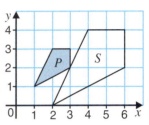

4 Copy triangle A onto squared paper.

Enlarge triangle A by scale factor $\frac{1}{2}$, centre O.

Edexcel

5 Copy triangle A onto squared paper.

Enlarge triangle A by the scale factor $\frac{1}{3}$ with centre the point $P(-7, 7)$.

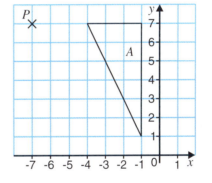

Edexcel

6 The diagram shows rectangles **A**, **B** and **C**.

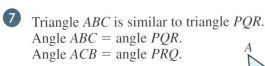
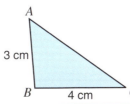
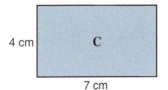

(a) Explain why rectangles **A** and **C** are **not** similar.
(b) Rectangles **A** and **B** are similar. Work out the length of rectangle **B**.

7 Triangle ABC is similar to triangle PQR.
Angle ABC = angle PQR.
Angle ACB = angle PRQ.

Calculate the length of
(a) PQ,   (b) AC.

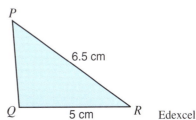

Edexcel

SECTION 32 — Pythagoras' Theorem

What you need to know

- The longest side in a right-angled triangle is called the **hypotenuse**.
- The **Theorem of Pythagoras** states:
  "In any right-angled triangle the square on the hypotenuse is equal to the sum of the squares on the other two sides."
  $$a^2 = b^2 + c^2$$

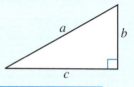

- When we know the lengths of two sides of a right-angled triangle, we can use the Theorem of Pythagoras to find the length of the third side.

$a^2 = b^2 + c^2$
Rearranging gives: $b^2 = a^2 - c^2$
$c^2 = a^2 - b^2$

Eg 1 Calculate the length of side a.

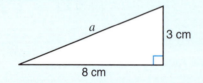

$a^2 = b^2 + c^2$
$a^2 = 8^2 + 3^2$
$a^2 = 64 + 9 = 73$
$a = \sqrt{73} = 8.544...$
$a = 8.5$ cm, correct to 1 d.p.

Eg 2 Calculate the length of side b.

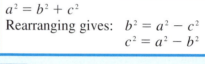

$b^2 = a^2 - c^2$
$b^2 = 9^2 - 7^2$
$b^2 = 81 - 49 = 32$
$b = \sqrt{32} = 5.656...$
$b = 5.7$ cm, correct to 1 d.p.

Exercise 32

Do not use a calculator for questions 1 and 2.

1 ABC is a right-angled triangle.
$AB = 5$ cm and $AC = 12$ cm.
Calculate the length of BC.

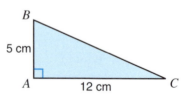

2

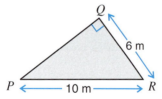

The diagram shows the cross-section of the roof of a house.
The width of the house, PR, is 10 m.
$QR = 6$ m and angle $PQR = 90°$.
Calculate the length of PQ.

3 The diagram shows a rectangular sheet of paper.
The paper is 20 cm wide and the diagonal, d, is 35 cm.

Calculate the length of the sheet of paper.

4 Calculate the length of the line joining the points $A(-2, -3)$ and $B(6, 1)$.

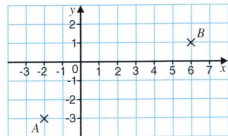

5 PQR is a right-angled triangle. $PQ = 5$ cm and $PR = 9$ cm.

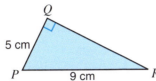

Calculate the length of QR and, hence, find the area of triangle PQR.

6 $AB = 19.5$ cm, $AC = 19.5$ cm and $BC = 16.4$ cm.
Angle $ADB = 90°$.
BDC is a straight line.

Calculate the length of AD.
Give your answer in centimetres, correct to 1 decimal place.

Edexcel

7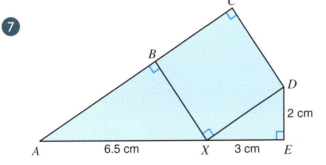

In the diagram, BCDX is a square.
AXE is a straight line with $AX = 6.5$ cm and $XE = 3$ cm.
$DE = 2$ cm.

(a) Calculate the area of BCDX.
(b) Calculate the length of AB, correct to one decimal place.

8 The diagram shows a sketch of a triangle.

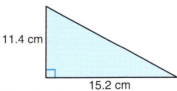

Work out the perimeter of the triangle.

Edexcel

9 ABCD is a rectangle. $AD = 5$ cm, $DC = 9$ cm and $EC = 6$ cm.

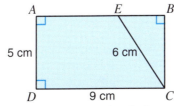

Calculate the length of AE, correct to one decimal place.

SECTION 33: Understanding and Using Measures

What you need to know

- The common units — both **metric** and **imperial** — used to measure **length**, **mass** and **capacity**.
- How to estimate measurements using sensible units and a suitable degree of accuracy.
- How to convert from one unit to another. This includes knowing the connection between one metric unit and another and the approximate equivalents between metric and imperial units.

Metric Units	Imperial Units	Conversions
Length 1 kilometre (km) = 1000 metres (m) 1 m = 100 centimetres (cm) 1 cm = 10 millimetres (mm) **Mass** 1 tonne (t) = 1000 kilograms (kg) 1 kg = 1000 grams (g) **Capacity and volume** 1 litre = 1000 millilitres (ml) 1 cm³ = 1 ml	**Length** 1 foot = 12 inches 1 yard = 3 feet **Mass** 1 pound = 16 ounces 14 pounds = 1 stone **Capacity and volume** 1 gallon = 8 pints	**Length** 5 miles is about 8 km 1 inch is about 2.5 cm 1 foot is about 30 cm **Mass** 1 kg is about 2.2 pounds **Capacity and volume** 1 litre is about 1.75 pints 1 gallon is about 4.5 litres

- How to change between units of area. For example $1 m^2 = 10\,000\, cm^2$.
- How to change between units of volume. For example $1 m^3 = 1\,000\,000\, cm^3$.
- You should be able to solve problems involving different units.

  Eg 1 A tank holds 6 gallons of water.
  How many litres is this? $6 \times 4.5 = 27$ litres

  Eg 2 A cuboid measures 1.5 m by 90 cm by 80 cm.
  Calculate the volume of the cuboid, in m³. $1.5 \times 0.9 \times 0.8 = 1.08\, m^3$

- Be able to read scales accurately.

  Eg 3 Part of a scale is shown.
  It measures weight in grams.
  What weight is shown by the arrow?

  The arrow shows 27 grams.

- Be able to recognise limitations on the accuracy of measurements.
  A measurement given to the nearest whole unit may be inaccurate by one half of a unit in either direction.

  Eg 4 A road is 400 m long, to the nearest 10 m.
  Between what lengths is the actual length of the road?
  Actual length = 400 m ± 5 m   395 m ≤ actual length < 405 m

- By analysing the **dimensions** of a formula it is possible to decide whether a given formula represents a **length** (dimension 1), an **area** (dimension 2) or a **volume** (dimension 3).

  Eg 5 p, q, r and s represent lengths.
  By using dimensions, decide whether the expression $pq + qr + rs$ could represent a perimeter, an area or a volume.
  Writing $pq + qr + rs$ using dimensions:
  $$L \times L + L \times L + L \times L = L^2 + L^2 + L^2 = 3L^2$$
  So, $pq + qr + rs$ has dimension 2 and could represent an area.

Exercise 33

Do not use a calculator for questions 1 to 6.

1 What value is shown by the pointer on each of these diagrams?
(a)  (b)  (c)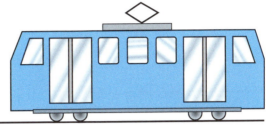

2 Write down the name of a unit which is used to measure
(a) the length of a garden,
(b) the amount of petrol in a car's petrol tank,
(c) the area of a school playing field,
(d) the weight of a calculator.
Edexcel

3 The diagram shows a man standing next to a tram. The man is of average height. Estimate the length of the tram. Give your answer in metres.
Edexcel

4 (a) How many metres are there in 4 kilometres?
(b) How many miles are the same as 4 kilometres?

5 The tank in Laura's car holds 12 gallons of petrol. How many litres is 12 gallons?

6 Fred buys some apples. They weigh 3.65 kilograms. Work out the approximate weight of the apples in pounds.
Edexcel

7 (a) A towel measures 150 cm by 90 cm. Calculate the area of the towel in square metres.
(b) Change $0.2\,m^3$ to cm^3.

8 Last year Felicity drove 2760 miles on business.
Her car does 38 miles per gallon. Petrol costs 89 pence per litre.
She is given a car allowance of 25 pence per kilometre.
How much of her car allowance is left after paying for her petrol?
Give your answer to the nearest £.

9 The length of Andy's pencil is 170 mm, correct to the nearest 10 mm.
What is the minimum length of the pencil?

10 The distance between two railway stations is recorded as 92 km, measured correct to the nearest kilometre. Let the actual distance be d km.
(a) Write down the least possible value for d.
(b) Copy and complete the inequality: $\ldots \leq d < \ldots$
Edexcel

11 Some of the expressions shown in the table below can be used to calculate areas or volumes of various shapes.
π and 2 are numbers which have no dimensions.
The letters r, b and h represent lengths.

| $2\pi r$ | πr^2 | $2bh$ | πr^3 | $b^2 h$ | $r^2 + b^3$ |

(a) Which of these expressions can be used to calculate an area?
(b) Which of these expressions can be used to calculate a volume?
Edexcel

Shape, Space and Measures
Non-calculator Paper

Do not use a calculator for this exercise.

1 (a) Copy the diagram.
Draw a line from the point C perpendicular to the line AB.
(b) Sketch a cylinder.

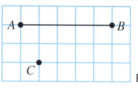

Edexcel

2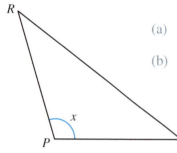

(a) Measure the length of RQ.
Write your answer in cm.
(b) (i) Measure and write down the size of the angle marked x.
(ii) Write down the special name for this type of angle.

Edexcel

3 The diagram shows some 3-dimensional shapes.

(a) How many edges has shape **A**?
(b) How many faces has shape **B**?
(c) What is the mathematical name for shape **C**?

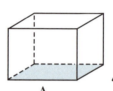

A B C

4 Each small square on the grid has a side of 1 cm.

(a) Work out the area of the shaded shape.
(b) Work out the perimeter of the shaded shape.

Not full size

Edexcel

5 In which compass direction is

(a) the Post Office from the Cinema,
(b) the Cinema from the Church?

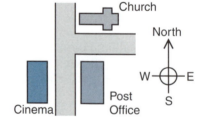

Edexcel

6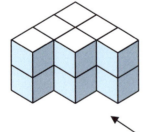

This solid has been made using 1 cm cubes.

(a) What is the volume of the solid?
(b) (i) Draw the plan of the solid.
(ii) Draw the elevation of the solid from the direction shown by the arrow.

7 Find the angles marked with letters. Give a reason for each of your answers.
(a) 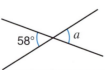 (b) 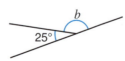 (c)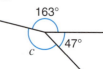

82

8 Here are 4 shapes labelled **A** to **D**.

 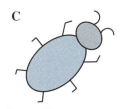 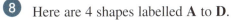 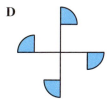

   (a) (i) Copy the diagrams and draw in any lines of symmetry on the shapes.
       (ii) Explain how you could check whether or not a line of symmetry was correct.
   (b) Write **TRUE** or **FALSE** for each of the following statements.
       (i) Shape **A** has rotational symmetry of order 2 or more.
       (ii) Shape **B** has rotational symmetry of order 2 or more.
       (iii) Shape **C** has rotational symmetry of order 2 or more.
       (iv) Shape **D** has rotational symmetry of order 2 or more.
                                                                                              Edexcel

9 The diagram shows a pyramid with a square base.
The base of the pyramid is a square with edges of length 6 cm.
The length of each sloping edge of the pyramid is 5 cm.

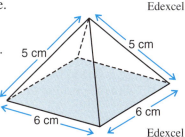

   (a) Make a sketch of a suitable net for the pyramid.
   (b) Make an accurate full-size drawing of one of the
       triangular faces of the pyramid.
                                                                                              Edexcel

10 Find the size of the angles a, b and c. Give a reason for each of your answers.

   (a) 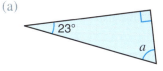   (b)    (c)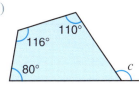

11 (a) Draw a square, a rhombus and a kite. Mark equal sides, parallel sides and equal angles.
   (b) Which quadrilaterals have four equal angles?
   (c) A rhombus is a special type of parallelogram as it possesses **all** the properties of a
       parallelogram. Which other special types of quadrilateral can a rhombus be?
                                                                                  Edexcel

12 Two hospitals are 20 miles apart.
What is the distance between the hospitals in kilometres?

13 This dial shows how much petrol is in the petrol tank of a car.
The full petrol tank holds 40 litres.
Estimate how many litres of petrol are in the petrol tank.

                                                                                   Edexcel

14 Work out the area of each shape.

   (a) 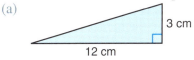   (b)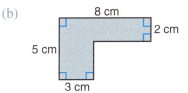

15 Triangle *ABC* is mapped onto triangle *PQR*, by an enlargement,
centre *O*, scale factor 3.
Copy the diagram and draw triangle *PQR*.

16 (a) Work out the size of an exterior angle of a regular pentagon.

The area of a pentagon is 8560 mm².
   (b) Change 8560 mm² to cm².
                                                                                     Edexcel

17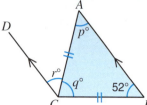

AC = BC.
AB is parallel to DC. Angle ABC = 52°.

(a) Work out the value of (i) p, (ii) q.

The angles marked p° and r° are equal.
(b) What geometrical name is given to this type of equal angles?

Edexcel

18 The scale drawing shows the positions of an airport tower, T, and a radio mast, M.
1 cm on the diagram represents 20 km.
(a) (i) Measure, in centimetres, the distance TM.
(ii) Work out the distance in km of the airport tower from the radio mast.
(b) (i) Measure and write down the bearing of the airport tower from the radio mast.
(ii) Write down the bearing of the radio mast from the airport tower.

Copy the diagram.
A plane is 80 km from the radio mast on a bearing of 220°.
(c) Plot the position of the plane on your diagram, using a scale of 1 cm to 20 km.

Edexcel

19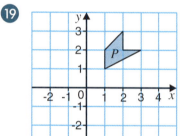

Copy the diagram onto squared paper.

(a) P is mapped onto Q by an enlargement, scale factor 2, centre (−1, 3). Draw and label Q.

(b) P is mapped onto R by a translation with vector $\begin{pmatrix} -3 \\ 2 \end{pmatrix}$. Draw and label R.

(c) P is mapped onto S by a rotation through 90° clockwise, about (1, 0). Draw and label S.

20 Work out the length of BC.

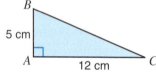

21 A circle has an area of 49π cm².
Calculate the circumference of the circle in terms of π.

22 Simone made a scale model of a "hot rod" car on a scale of 1 to 12.5.
The height of the model car is 10 cm.
(a) Work out the height of the real car.

The length of the real car is 5 m.
(b) Work out the length of the model car. Give your answer in centimetres.

The angle the windscreen makes with the bonnet on the real car is 140°.
(c) What is the angle the windscreen makes with the bonnet on the model car?

The width of the windscreen in the real car is 119 cm, correct to the nearest centimetre.
(d) Write down the smallest length this measurement could be.

Edexcel

23 The following formulae represent certain quantities connected with containers, where *a*, *b* and *c* are dimensions.

$$\pi a \qquad abc \qquad \sqrt{a^2 - c^2} \qquad \pi a^2 b \qquad 2(a + b + c)$$

(a) Explain why *abc* represents a volume.
(b) Which of these formulae represent lengths?

24 Calculate the volume of this triangular prism.

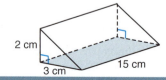

Shape, Space and Measures Calculator Paper

You may use a calculator for this exercise.

1 (a) Measure the length of the line.

The line is to be the **diameter** of a circle.
(b) Draw a copy of the line and mark the centre of your circle with a cross.
(c) Draw the circle.

Edexcel

2 (a) Which of these weights are the same?
8000 g   80 kg   800 g   8 kg   0.08 kg
(b) Which of these lengths is the longest?
0.2 km   20 m   2000 mm   200 cm
(c) The scales show weights in kilograms.
Write down the weight of the pears.

3

Here is an accurate drawing of a shape.
Copy the shape.

(a) Draw the line of symmetry on your shape.
(b) Write down the special name for this shape.
(c) On your shape, mark with an X, an obtuse angle.

Edexcel

4 Copy the diagram.

Draw the reflection of the shape in the mirror line.

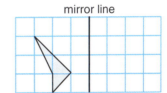

5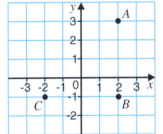

The diagram shows points A, B and C.

(a) What are the coordinates of A?
(b) What are the coordinates of C?
(c) ABCD is a square.
What are the coordinates of D?

6 Here are 8 shapes.

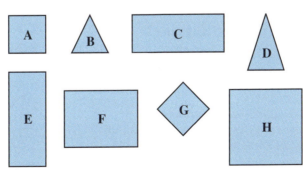

Write down the letters of two **different** pairs of congruent shapes.

Edexcel

7 (a) What special name is given to this polygon?

(b) Show how this shape will tessellate.
You should draw at least 8 shapes.

Edexcel

8. This diagram is wrong.
   Explain why.

   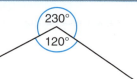

   Edexcel

9. Colin is 5 feet 10 inches tall and weighs 11 stones.
   On a medical form he is asked to give his height in centimetres and his weight in kilograms.
   What values should he give?

10. The diagram shows the positions of shapes *P*, *Q*, *R* and *S*.

    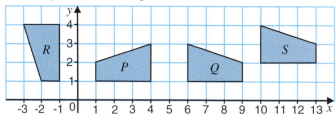

    Describe the single transformation which takes:
    (a) *P* onto *Q*,   (b) *P* onto *R*,   (c) *Q* onto *S*.

11. Find the size of the angles *a*, *b*, *c* and *d*.
    (a)   (b)

12. (a) Copy the diagram.
       Shade **one** square so that the shape has exactly **one** line of symmetry.
    (b) Make **another** copy of the diagram.
       Shade **one** square so that the shape has rotational symmetry of order 2.

    Edexcel

13. (a) A cuboid measures 2 cm by 2.5 cm by 4 cm.
       (i) Draw an accurate net of the cuboid.
       (ii) Calculate the total surface area of the cuboid.
    (b) Another cuboid has a volume of 50 cm³. The base of the cuboid measures 4 cm by 5 cm.
       Calculate the height of the cuboid.

14. Shape *A* has a line of symmetry.
    (a) Write down the equation of this line of symmetry.

    Copy the diagram.
    (b) Enlarge shape *A* by scale factor 2, centre *O*, to give shape *B*.
       Draw and label shape *B*.

    Edexcel

15. The diagram shows a square-based pyramid.
    (a) How many planes of symmetry has the pyramid?
    (b) How many axes of symmetry has the pyramid?

    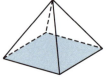

16. The radius of a circle is 6.4 cm.
    Work out the circumference of this circle.

    Edexcel

17. Ben fills a container with boxes. Each box is a cube of side 0.5 m.
    The container is a cuboid of length 9 m, width 4 m and height 3 m.
    Work out how many boxes will fit exactly into the container.

    Edexcel

18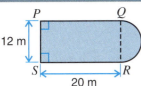
The diagram shows the plan of a swimming pool.
The arc QR is a semi-circle.
PS = 12 m and PQ = RS = 20 m.

Calculate the area of the surface of the pool.

19 Plot the points P (1, 4) and Q (6, 2).
Construct accurately the locus of all points which are equidistant from P and Q.   *Edexcel*

20 The diagram shows the angle formed when three regular polygons are placed together, as shown.

(a) Explain why angle a is 120°.
(b) Work out the size of the angle marked b.

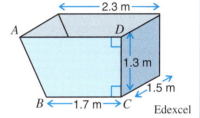

21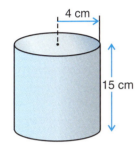
A can of drink is in the shape of a cylinder.
The can has a radius of 4 cm and a height of 15 cm.

Calculate the volume of the cylinder.

Edexcel

22 A skip is in the shape of a prism with cross-section ABCD.
AD = 2.3 m, DC = 1.3 m and BC = 1.7 m.
The width of the skip is 1.5 m.

(a) Calculate the area of the shape ABCD.
(b) Calculate the volume of the skip.

Edexcel

23 Three oil rigs, X, Y and Z, are supplied by boats from port P.
X is 15 km from P on a bearing of 050°.
Y is 20 km from P on a bearing of 110°.
Z is equidistant from X and Y and 30 km from P.
(a) By using a scale of 1 cm to represent 5 km, draw an accurate diagram to show the positions of P, X, Y and Z.
(b) Use your diagram to find
    (i) the bearing of Y from Z,   (ii) the distance, in kilometres, of Y from Z.

24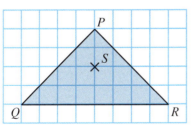
Triangle PQR is drawn on the grid.
The point S is also shown.

Copy triangle PQR onto squared paper and enlarge the triangle PQR using a scale factor of $\frac{1}{2}$.
Use S as the centre of enlargement.

Edexcel

25 Ballymena is due West of Larne.
Woodburn is 15 km due South of Larne.
Ballymena is 32 km from Woodburn.

Calculate the distance of Larne from Ballymena.

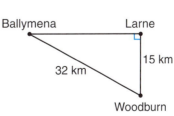

26 The distance of a helicopter from the radio mast is 70 km, correct to the nearest kilometre.
Write down
(a) the maximum distance the helicopter could be from the radio mast,
(b) the minimum distance the helicopter could be from the radio mast.

Edexcel

SECTION 34 — Collection and Organisation of Data

What you need to know

- **Primary data** is data collected by an individual or organisation to use for a particular purpose. Primary data is obtained from experiments, investigations, surveys and by using questionnaires.
- **Secondary data** is data which is already available or has been collected by someone else for a different purpose.
  Sources of secondary data include the Annual Abstract of Statistics, Social Trends and the Internet.
- **Qualitative** data – Data which can only be described in words.   E.g. Colour of cars.
- **Quantitative** data – Data that has a numerical value.
  Quantitative data is either **discrete** or **continuous**.
  Discrete data can only take certain values.   E.g. Numbers of cars in car parks.
  Continuous data has no exact value and is measurable.   E.g. Weights of cars.
- **Data Collection Sheets** – Used to record data during a survey.
- **Tally** – A way of recording each item of data on a data collection sheet.
  A group of five is recorded as ||||.
- **Frequency Table** – A way of collating the information recorded on a data collection sheet.
- **Grouped Frequency Table** – Used for continuous data or for discrete data when a lot of data has to be recorded.
- **Database** – A collection of data.
- **Class Interval** – The width of the groups used in a grouped frequency distribution.
- **Questionnaire** – A set of questions used to collect data for a survey.
  Questionnaires should:
  (1) use simple language,
  (2) ask short questions which can be answered precisely,
  (3) provide tick boxes,
  (4) avoid open-ended questions,
  (5) avoid leading questions,
  (6) ask questions in a logical order.
- **Hypothesis** – A hypothesis is a statement which may or may not be true.
- When information is required about a large group of people it is not always possible to survey everyone and only a **sample** may be asked.
  The sample chosen should be large enough to make the results meaningful and representative of the whole group (population) or the results may be **biased**.
- **Two-way Tables** – A way of illustrating two features of a survey.

Exercise 34

1 Harry wants to find out how people travel to work.
  (a) (i) Design an observation sheet for Harry to record data.
      (ii) Complete your observation sheet by inventing data for 20 people.
  (b) Harry decides to stand outside the bus station to collect his data.
      Give a reason why this is not a suitable place to carry out the survey.

2 The table shows information about pupils in the same class at a school.

Name	Gender	Month of birth	Day of birth
Corrin	F	June	Monday
Daniel	M	March	Thursday
Laila	F	May	Friday
Ria	F	March	Tuesday
Miles	M	April	Tuesday

(a) Who was born in May?
(b) Who was born on a Tuesday in March?
(c) Which of these pupils is most likely to be the youngest?
    Give a reason for your answer.

3 Tayfan is organising a skiing holiday to Italy for his friends.
They can go to Cervinia, Livigno or Tonale.
He asks each of his friends which resort they would like to go to and records the answers in his notebook.

```
Cervinia  Cervinia  Livigno   Tonale
Tonale    Tonale    Livigno   Cervinia
Livigno   Cervinia  Tonale    Tonale
Cervinia  Livigno   Tonale    Livigno
Tonale    Cervinia  Livigno   Tonale
Livigno   Tonale    Cervinia
```

Show a better way of recording this information.

4 Meeta is doing a survey about sport. She asks the question,

"Do you play football, rugby or hockey?"

(a) Give a reason why this is not a suitable question.
(b) Write a similar question which is suitable.

5 Here are the weights, in kilograms, of 30 students.

```
45  52  56  65  34  45  67  65  34  45  65  87  45  34  56
54  45  67  84  45  67  45  56  76  57  84  35  64  58  60
```

(a) Copy and complete the frequency table below using a class interval of 10, starting at 30.

Weight range (w kg)	Tally	Frequency
$30 \leq w < 40$		

(b) Which class interval has the highest frequency?

Edexcel

6 50 pupils are going on an educational visit. The pupils have to choose to go to one of:
the Theatre or **the Art Gallery** or **the Science Museum**.
23 of the pupils are boys.
11 of the girls choose to visit the theatre.
9 of the girls choose to visit the art gallery.
13 of the boys choose to visit the science museum.

	Theatre	Art Gallery	Science Museum	Totals
Girls	11	9		
Boys			13	23
Totals	19		20	50

(a) Copy and complete the table.
(b) How many of the girls choose to visit the science museum?

Edexcel

7 Each student at Redmond School studies one foreign language.
Students can choose from French, German and Spanish.
The headteacher wants to show how many boys and how many girls study each language.
(a) Draw a two-way table the headteacher could use to show this information.
(b) 23 boys study French. Write the number 23 in the correct place in your table. *Edexcel*

8 Jamie is investigating the use made of his college library. Here is part of his questionnaire:

> **Library Questionnaire**
> 1. How old are you? ....

(a) (i) Give a reason why this question is unsuitable.
(ii) Rewrite the question so that it could be included.
(b) Jamie asks the librarian to give the questionnaires to students when they borrow books.
(i) Give reasons why this sample may be biased.
(ii) Suggest a better way of giving out the questionnaires.

9 Martin, the local Youth Centre leader, wishes to know why attendance at the Youth Centre is less than at the same time last year. He thinks that it could be due to a number of changes that occurred during the course of the year. These changes were:

the opening hours changed,
a new sports centre opened nearby,
some of the older members started bullying the younger members.

Design a suitable question, that is easily answered, to find out why people do not attend the Youth Centre. *Edexcel*

10 This sample was used to investigate the claim: **"Women do more exercise than men."**

	Age (years)			
	16 to 21	22 to 45	46 to 65	Over 65
Male	5	5	13	7
Female	25	35	0	0

Give three reasons why the sample is biased.

11 The table shows the results of a survey of 500 people.

	Can drive	Cannot drive
Men	180	20
Women	240	60

A newspaper headline states: **Survey shows that more women can drive than men.**
Do the results of the survey support this headline? Give a reason for your answer.

12 The two-way table shows the results of a survey of the number of cats and the number of dogs people have as pets.

		Number of cats			
		0	1	2	3
Number of dogs	0	21	9	3	0
	1	5	4	2	0
	2	2	1	0	1
	3	1	1	0	0

(a) How many people have one dog **and** two cats as pets?
(b) A magazine article stated, *"Cats are more popular than dogs as pets."*
Does this survey support that claim? Give a reason for your answer.
(c) How many dogs did these people have altogether?

SECTION 35 — Pictograms and Bar Charts

What you need to know

- **Pictogram**. Symbols are used to represent information.
  Each symbol can represent one or more items of data.

  Eg 1 A sports club has 45 members.
  Last Saturday, 15 played football, 13 played hockey and 17 played rugby.

  Draw a pictogram to show this information. Use ☆ = 5 members.

  Note: ⌁ represents 3 members
  ○ represents 2 members

- **Bar chart**. Used for data which can be counted.
  Often used to compare quantities of data in a distribution.
  The length of each bar represents frequency.
  The longest bar represents the **mode**.
  The difference between the largest and smallest variable is called the **range**.

  Bars can be drawn horizontally or vertically.
  Bars are the same width and there are gaps between bars.

- **Bar-line graph**. Instead of drawing bars, horizontal or vertical lines are drawn to show frequency.

  Eg 2 The graph shows the number of goals scored by a football team in 10 matches.

  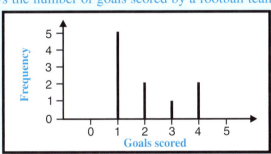

  (a) Which number of goals scored is the mode?
  (b) What is the range of the number of goals scored?

  (a) The tallest bar represents the mode. The mode is 1 goal.
  (b) The range is the difference between the largest and smallest number of goals scored.
      The range = 4 − 1 = 3

Exercise 35

1 The pictogram shows the number of parcels posted at the High Street Post Office on Monday, Tuesday and Wednesday.

(a) How many parcels were posted on
  (i) Monday,
  (ii) Tuesday?

25 parcels were posted on Thursday.
(b) Copy and complete the pictogram.

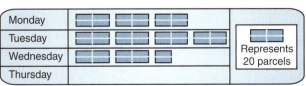

Edexcel

2 The bar chart shows information about the favourite drink of each student in a class.

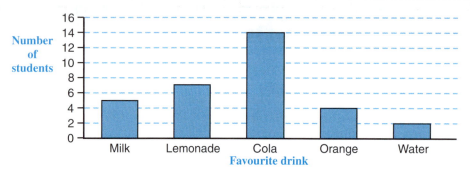

(a) Which was the favourite drink of the greatest number of students?
(b) Write down the number of students whose favourite drink was lemonade.
(c) Work out the **total** number of students in the class.

Edexcel

3 Francis asks his friends to name their favourite flavour of yogurt.
The results are shown in the tally chart.

(a) How many friends said strawberry?
(b) What percentage said vanilla?
(c) Draw a pictogram to show Francis's results.

Use the symbol 👤 to represent 5 friends.

Flavour	Tally
Strawberry	|||| |||
Vanilla	||||
Other	|||| |||| |||

4 Robin carried out a traffic survey.
The table shows how many buses, cars, bicycles, vans and lorries he saw.

Type of vehicle	Bus	Car	Bicycle	Van	Lorry
Number of vehicles	10	22	4	8	14

Use this information to draw a bar chart.

Edexcel

5 Causeway Hockey Club have a hockey team for men and a hockey team for women.
The bar chart shows the number of goals scored in matches played by these teams last season.

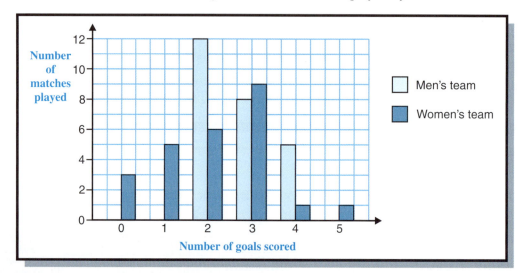

(a) For the men's team, find the range and mode in the number of goals scored.
(b) Compare and comment on the goals scored by these teams last season.

SECTION 36 — Averages and Range

What you need to know

- There are three types of **average**: the **mode**, the **median** and the **mean**.
  The **mode** is the most common value.
  The **median** is the middle value (or the mean of the two middle values) when the values are arranged in order of size.
  The **Mean** = $\dfrac{\text{Total of all values}}{\text{Number of values}}$

- The **range** is a measure of **spread**, and is the difference between the highest and lowest values.

  Eg 1 The number of text messages received by 7 students on Saturday is shown.

  2   4   3   4   4   3   2

  Find (a) the mode,   (b) the median,   (c) the mean,   (d) the range.

  (a) The mode is 4.

  (b) 2   2   3   ③   4   4   4   The median is 3.

  (c) The mean = $\dfrac{2+4+3+4+4+3+2}{7} = \dfrac{22}{7} = 3.14\ldots = 3.1$, correct to 1 d.p.

  (d) The range = $4 - 2 = 2$

- To find the mean of a **frequency distribution** use:

  $$\text{Mean} = \dfrac{\text{Total of all values}}{\text{Number of values}} = \dfrac{\Sigma fx}{\Sigma f}$$

  Eg 2 The table shows the number of stamps on some parcels.

Number of stamps	1	2	3	4
Number of parcels	5	6	9	4

  Find the mean number of stamps per parcel.

  Mean = $\dfrac{\text{Total number of stamps}}{\text{Number of parcels}} = \dfrac{1\times 5 + 2\times 6 + 3\times 9 + 4\times 4}{5+6+9+4} = \dfrac{60}{24} = 2.5$

- To find the mean of a **grouped frequency distribution**, first find the value of the midpoint of each class.
  Then use:

  $$\text{Estimated mean} = \dfrac{\text{Total of all values}}{\text{Number of values}} = \dfrac{\Sigma fx}{\Sigma f}$$

  Eg 3 The table shows the weights of some parcels.

Weight (w grams)	Frequency
$100 \leqslant w < 200$	7
$200 \leqslant w < 300$	11
$300 \leqslant w < 400$	19
$400 \leqslant w < 500$	3

  Calculate an estimate of the mean weight of these parcels.

  Mean = $\dfrac{\Sigma fx}{\Sigma f} = \dfrac{150 \times 7 + 250 \times 11 + 350 \times 19 + 450 \times 3}{7 + 11 + 19 + 3} = \dfrac{11\,800}{40} = 295$ grams

- You should be able to choose the best average to use in different situations:
  - When the most **popular** value is wanted use the **mode**.
  - When **half** of the values have to be above the average use the **median**.
  - When a **typical** value is wanted use either the **mode** or the **median**.
  - When all the **actual** values have to be taken into account use the **mean**.
  - When the average should not be distorted by a few very small or very large values do **not** use the mean.

Exercise 36

Do not use a calculator for questions 1 to 3.

1. Nine students were asked to estimate the length of this line, correct to the nearest centimetre.

   The estimates the students made are shown.

   8   10   10   10   11   12   12   14   15

   (a) What is the range in their estimates?
   (b) Which estimate is the mode?
   (c) Which estimate is the median?
   (d) Work out the mean of their estimates.

2. The prices paid for eight different meals at a restaurant are:

   £10   £9   £9.50   £12   £20   £11.50   £11   £9

   (a) Which price is the mode?
   (b) Find the median price.
   (c) Calculate the mean price.
   (d) Which of these averages best describes the average price paid for a meal? Give a reason for your answer.

3. Some students took a mental arithmetic test.
   Information about their marks is shown in the table.

Mark	4	5	6	7	8	9	10
Frequency	2	1	2	4	7	10	3

   (a) Work out how many students took the test.
   (b) Write down the modal mark.

   24 students had a higher mark than Caroline.
   (c) Work out Caroline's mark.
   (d) Find the median mark.
   (e) Work out the range of the marks.

   Edexcel

4. (a) The number of hours of sunshine each day last week is shown.

Monday	Tuesday	Wednesday	Thursday	Friday	Saturday	Sunday
5.3	6.4	3.7	4.8	7.5	8.6	5.7

   (i) What is the range in the number of hours of sunshine each day?
   (ii) Work out the mean number of hours of sunshine each day.

   (b) In the same week last year, the range in the number of hours of sunshine each day was 9 hours and the mean was 3.5 hours.
   Compare the number of hours of sunshine each day in these two weeks.

5. 20 students took part in a competition.
   The frequency table shows the points they scored.

Points scored	1	2	3
Frequency	9	4	7

   Work out the total number of points scored by the 20 students.

   Edexcel

6 Helen and Reg play ten-pin bowling.
The graph shows their scores for the first 10 frames.

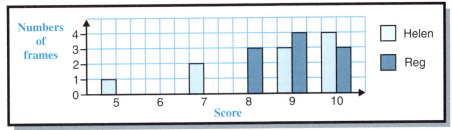

(a) What is the range in the scores for Helen?
(b) Find the mean of the scores for Reg.
(c) Reg says, "My average score is higher than Helen's."
Helen says, "My average score is higher than Reg's."
A friend says, "Your average scores are both the same."
Which average is being used by each person?
Show your working.

7 Darren throws a dice 60 times. His results are shown.

Score	1	2	3	4	5	6
Frequency	12	10	9	11	10	8

(a) For these results, find
  (i) the mode,   (ii) the median,   (iii) the mean.
(b) Darren throws the dice again and scores a 6.
Which of the averages he has found will not change?

8 75 boys took part in a darts competition.
Each boy threw darts until he hit the centre of the dartboard.
The numbers of darts thrown by the boys are grouped in this frequency table.

Number of darts thrown	Frequency
1 to 5	10
6 to 10	17
11 to 15	12
16 to 20	4
21 to 25	12
26 to 30	20

(a) Work out the class interval which contains the median.
(b) Work out an estimate for the mean number of darts thrown by each boy.

Edexcel

9 The table shows the number of students in three groups attending Maths City High School last Monday. No student belonged to more than one group.

Group	A	B	C
Number of students	135	225	200

Mrs Allen carried out a survey about the students' travelling times from home to school last Monday.
Mrs Allen worked out that:

- the mean time for Group *A* students was 24 minutes,
- the mean time for Group *B* students was 32 minutes,
- the mean time for Group *C* students was the same as the mean time for all 560 students.

Work out the mean time for all 560 students.

Edexcel

Section 37: Pie Charts and Stem and Leaf Diagrams

What you need to know

- **Pie chart**. Used for data which can be counted.
  Often used to compare proportions of data, usually with the total.
  The whole circle represents all the data.
  The size of each sector represents the frequency of data in that sector.
  The largest sector represents the **mode**.

  Eg 1 The pie chart shows the makes of 120 cars.
  (a) Which make of car is the mode?
  (b) How many of the cars are Ford?

  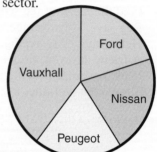

  (a) The sector representing Vauxhall is the largest.
  Therefore, Vauxhall is the mode.
  (b) The angle of the sector representing Ford is 72°.
  The number of Ford cars $= \frac{72}{360} \times 120 = 24$

- **Stem and leaf diagrams**. Used to represent data in its original form.
  Data is split into two parts.
  The part with the higher place value is the stem.   E.g. 15 = stem 1, leaf 5.
  A key is given to show the value of the data.   E.g. 3 | 4 means 3.4, etc.
  The data is shown in numerical order on the diagram.   E.g. 2 | 3 5 9 represents 23, 25, 29.

  Back to back stem and leaf diagrams can be used to compare two sets of data.

  Eg 2 The times, in seconds, taken by 10 students to complete a puzzle are shown.
      9   23   17   20   12   11   24   12   10   26
  Construct a stem and leaf diagram to represent this information.

                    2 | 0 means 20 seconds
      0 | 9
      1 | 0 1 2 2 7
      2 | 0 3 4 6

Exercise 37

1 The stem and leaf diagram shows the highest November temperature recorded in 12 European countries last year.

                  0 | 7 means 7°C
    0 | 7 9
    1 | 0 3 4 4 4 7 8
    2 | 0 1 2

(a) How many countries are included?
(b) What is the maximum temperature recorded?
(c) Which temperature is the mode?
(d) When the temperature in another European country is included in the data, the range increases by 2°C.
What was the temperature in that country?
Explain your answer.

2 The pie chart shows how Jenny spends her monthly income.
Jenny spends £180 a month on food.

(a) Work out Jenny's monthly income.

(b) Work out how much rent Jenny pays each month.

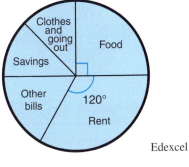

Edexcel

3 In a survey, some students were asked what their favourite leisure activity was.
Their answers were used to draw this pie chart.

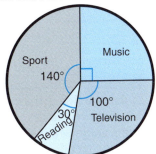

(a) Write down the fraction of the students who answered "Television".
Write your answer in its simplest form.

18 students answered "Music".

(b) Work out the number of students who took part in the survey.

Edexcel

4 40 passengers at Gatwick Airport were asked which country they were flying to.
Here is a frequency table which shows that information.

Country	USA	France	Spain	Greece
Number of passengers	14	10	11	5

Draw an accurate pie chart to show this information.

Edexcel

5 The number of text messages Anila sent each day in the last two weeks is shown.

7   12   10   5   21   11   9   2   17   3   5   13   20   15

(a) Construct a stem and leaf diagram to show this information.

(b) What is the range in the number of text messages Anila sent each day?

6 The pie chart gives information about the bills paid by a Water Company.

(a) Work out the size of the angle representing Wages.

The Water Company spent £18 000 on Materials.

(b) Work out the amount it spent on Rates.

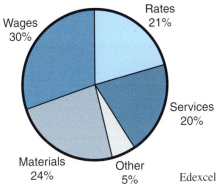

Edexcel

7 Twenty children were asked to estimate the length of a leaf.
Their estimates, in centimetres, are:

Boys									
4.5	5.0	4.0	3.5	4.0	4.5	5.0	4.5	3.5	4.5

Girls									
4.5	5.0	3.5	4.0	5.5	3.5	4.5	3.5	3.0	2.5

(a) Construct a back to back stem and leaf diagram to represent this information.

(b) Compare and comment on the estimates of these boys and girls.

SECTION 38 Time Series and Frequency Diagrams

What you need to know

- A **time series** is a set of readings taken at time intervals.
- A **line graph** is used to show a time series.

  Eg 1 The table shows the temperature of a patient taken every half-hour.

Time	0930	1000	1030	1100	1130	1200
Temperature °C	36.9	37.1	37.6	37.2	36.5	37.0

  (a) Draw a line graph to illustrate the data.
  (b) Estimate the patient's temperature at 1115.

  (a)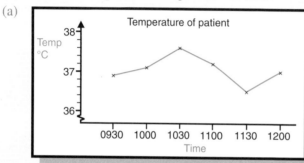

  To draw a line graph:
  Plot the given values.
  Points are joined by lines to show the **trend**.

  Only the plotted points represent **actual values**.
  The lines show the **trend** and can be used to **estimate values**.

  (b) 36.8°C

- **Histogram.** Used to illustrate **grouped frequency distributions.**
  The horizontal axis is a continuous scale.
- **Frequency polygon.** Used to illustrate grouped frequency distributions.
  Often used to compare two or more distributions on the same diagram.
  Frequencies are plotted at the midpoints of the class intervals and joined with straight lines.
  The horizontal axis is a continuous scale.

  Eg 2 The frequency distribution of the heights of some boys is shown.

Height (h cm)	$130 \leq h < 140$	$140 \leq h < 150$	$150 \leq h < 160$	$160 \leq h < 170$	$170 \leq h < 180$
Frequency	1	7	12	9	3

  Draw a histogram and a frequency polygon to illustrate the data.

  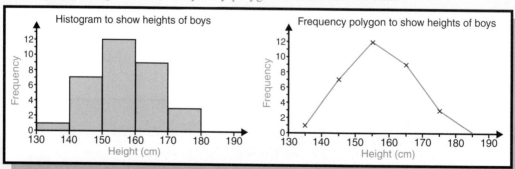

- **Misleading graphs.** Graphs may be misleading if:
  the scales are not labelled, the scales are not uniform, the frequency does not begin at zero.

Exercise 38

1. On Sunday, Alfie records the outside temperature every two hours.
   The temperatures he recorded are shown in the table.

Time of day	0800	1000	1200	1400	1600	1800
Outside temperature (°C)	9	12	15	17	16	14

   (a) Draw a line graph to represent the data.
   (b) What is the range in the temperatures recorded?
   (c) (i) Use your graph to estimate the temperature at 1300.
       (ii) Explain why your answer in (c)(i) is an estimate.

2. Robin had a holiday job packing cheese.
   Each pack of cheese should weigh 500 grams.
   Robin checked the weights, in grams, of 30 packs of cheese. These are the results.

     512 506 503 506 499 506 507 499 500 504
     502 503 510 508 496 497 497 509 506 496
     496 499 497 498 507 511 503 493 498 491

   (a) Copy and complete the grouped frequency table for the weights.
   Use class intervals of 5 g.

Weight (w grams)	Tally	Frequency
$490 \leq w < 495$		

   (b) Draw a frequency diagram to represent the data.
   (c) State the modal class.
                                                                                                                                                              Edexcel

3. The table shows the frequency distribution of student absences for a year.

Absences (d days)	Frequency
$0 < d < 5$	4
$5 \leq d < 10$	6
$10 \leq d < 15$	8
$15 \leq d < 20$	5
$20 \leq d < 25$	4
$25 \leq d < 30$	3

   (a) Draw a frequency polygon for this frequency distribution.
   (b) Write down the class which contains the median.
   (c) What percentage of students were absent for 25 days or more?
                                                                                         Edexcel

4. The graph shows the time taken to score the first goal in 20 football matches.

   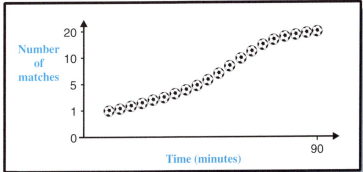

   Explain why the graph is misleading.

5. The table shows information about the heights of 40 bushes.

Height (h cm)	Frequency
$170 < h < 175$	5
$175 \leq h < 180$	18
$180 \leq h < 185$	12
$185 \leq h < 190$	4
$190 \leq h < 195$	1

(a) Draw a frequency graph for this information.
(b) In which class interval is the median height of the bushes?

Edexcel

6. The graph shows the age distribution of people in a nursing home.

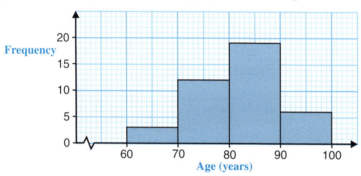

(a) Which age group is the modal class?
(b) How many people are in the nursing home?
(c) The table shows the age distribution of men in the home.

Age (a years)	$60 \leq a < 70$	$70 \leq a < 80$	$80 \leq a < 90$	$90 \leq a < 100$
Frequency	2	7	6	0

(i) Draw a frequency polygon to represent this information.
(ii) On the same diagram draw a frequency polygon to represent the age distribution of women in the home.
(iii) Compare and comment on the ages of men and women in the home.

7. The frequency polygon illustrates the age distribution of people taking part in a marathon.

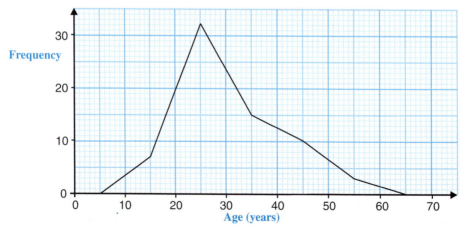

(a) How many people were under 20 years of age?
(b) How many people were over 50 years of age?
(c) How many people took part?

SECTION 39 — Scatter Graphs

What you need to know

- A **scatter graph** can be used to show the relationship between two sets of data.
- The relationship between two sets of data is referred to as **correlation**.
- You should be able to recognise **positive** and **negative** correlation. The correlation is stronger as points get closer to a straight line.
- When there is a relationship between two sets of data a **line of best fit** can be drawn on the scatter graph.
- **Perfect correlation** is when all the points lie on a straight line.
- The line of best fit can be used to **estimate** the value from one set of the data when the corresponding value of the other set is known.

Positive correlation   Negative correlation

Eg 1 The table shows the weights and heights of 10 girls.

Weight (kg)	33	36	37	39	40	42	45	45	48	48
Height (cm)	133	134	137	140	146	146	145	150	152	156

(a) Draw a scatter graph for the data. (b) What type of correlation is shown?
(c) Draw a line of best fit. (d) A girl weighs 50 kg. Estimate her height.

Mark a cross on the graph to show the weight and height of each girl.

(a)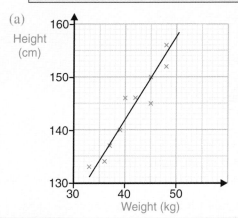

(b) Positive correlation.
(c) The line of best fit has been drawn, by eye, on the graph.

On a scatter graph:
The **slope** of the line of best fit shows the **trend** of the data.
The line of best fit does not have to go through the origin of the graph.

(d) 158 cm.
Read estimate where 50 kg meets line of best fit.

Exercise 39

1 Nine different models of car were tested to see how long it took each car to travel 500 metres from a standing start. The times, together with the size of each engine, are shown in the table.

Engine size cc	1000	1200	1250	1400	1450	1600	1800	1950	2000
Time (seconds)	26	23	23	21	21	19	18	16	14

(a) Use this information to draw a scatter graph.
(b) Describe the relationship between the time a car takes to travel 500 metres and the size of its engine.
(c) Draw a line of best fit on your scatter graph.
(d) Use your line of best fit to predict the time taken to travel 500 metres by a car with an engine size of 1900 cc.

Edexcel

2. The scatter graphs show the results of a survey given to people on holiday at a seaside resort.

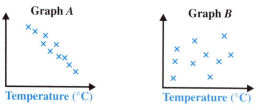
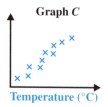

(a) Which scatter graph shows the temperature (°C) plotted against:
  (i) the number of people in the sea,
  (ii) the number of people with coats on,
  (iii) the amount of money people spend?
(b) Which scatter graph shows a positive correlation?

3. The scatter graph shows the results of candidates in two examinations in the same subject.

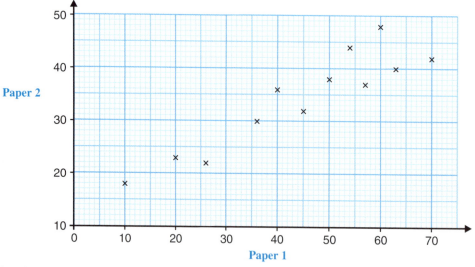

(a) One candidate scored 40 marks on Paper 1.
    What mark did this candidate score on Paper 2?
(b) One candidate scored 48 marks on Paper 2.
    What mark did this candidate score on Paper 1?
(c) Was the highest mark on both papers scored by the same candidate?
(d) Was the lowest mark on both papers scored by the same candidate?
(e) What type of correlation is there between the marks scored on the two exam papers?

4. On seven days, Helen recorded the time, in minutes, it took a 2 cm ice cube to melt.
She also recorded the temperature, in °C, on that day.
All of her results are shown in the table below.

Temperature (°C)	9	11.5	15	17	20	21	26
Time (minutes)	63	55	48	40	30	25	12.5

(a) Draw a scatter graph for the data.
(b) Describe the relationship between the temperature and the time it takes a 2 cm ice cube to melt.
(c) Draw a line of best fit on your scatter graph.
(d) Use your line of best fit to estimate the time it took for a 2 cm ice cube to melt when the temperature was 13°C.
(e) Use your line of best fit to estimate the temperature when a 2 cm ice cube took 19 minutes to melt.
(f) Explain why the line of best fit could not be used to estimate the time it took a 2 cm ice cube to melt when the temperature was 35°C.

Edexcel

SECTION 40 Probability

What you need to know

- **Probability** describes how likely or unlikely it is that an event will occur.
  Probabilities can be shown on a probability scale.

  ← Less likely   More likely →
  Impossible ———————————— Certain
  0            $\frac{1}{2}$ 1

  Probability **must** be written as a **fraction**, a **decimal** or a **percentage**.

- How to work out probabilities using **equally likely outcomes**.

  $$\text{The probability of an event} = \frac{\text{Number of outcomes in the event}}{\text{Total number of possible outcomes}}$$

  Eg 1 A box contains 7 red pens and 4 blue pens. A pen is taken from the box at random.
  What is the probability that the pen is blue?

  $$P(\text{blue}) = \frac{\text{Number of blue pens}}{\text{Total number of pens}} = \frac{4}{11}$$

  P(blue) stands for the probability that the pen is blue.

- How to estimate probabilities using **relative frequency**.

  $$\text{Relative frequency} = \frac{\text{Number of times the event happens in an experiment (or in a survey)}}{\text{Total number of trials in the experiment (or observations in the survey)}}$$

  Eg 2 A spinner is spun 20 times. The results are shown.

  4 1 3 1 4 2 2 4 3 3
  4 1 4 4 3 2 2 1 3 2

  What is the relative frequency of getting a 4?

  $$\text{Relative frequency} = \frac{\text{Number of 4's}}{\text{Number of spins}} = \frac{6}{20} = 0.3$$

  Relative frequency gives a better estimate of probability the larger the number of trials.

- How to use probabilities to **estimate** the number of times an event occurs in an **experiment** or **observation**.

  $$\text{Estimate} = \text{total number of trials (or observations)} \times \text{probability of event}$$

  Eg 3 1000 raffle tickets are sold. Alan buys some tickets.
  The probability that Alan wins first prize is $\frac{1}{50}$.
  How many tickets did Alan buy?   Number of tickets $= 1000 \times \frac{1}{50} = 20$

- **Mutually exclusive events** cannot occur at the same time.

  When A and B are mutually exclusive events: $P(A \text{ or } B) = P(A) + P(B)$

  Eg 4 A box contains red, green, blue and yellow counters.
  The table shows the probability of getting each colour.

Colour	Red	Green	Blue	Yellow
Probability	0.4	0.25	0.25	0.1

  A counter is taken from the box at random.
  What is the probability of getting a red or blue counter?
  $P(\text{Red or Blue}) = P(\text{Red}) + P(\text{Blue}) = 0.4 + 0.25 = 0.65$

> The probability of an event, A, **not happening** is: P(not A) = 1 − P(A)
>
> **Eg 5** Kathy takes a sweet from a bag at random.
> The probability that it is a toffee is 0.3.
> What is the probability that it is **not** a toffee?
>
> P(not toffee) = 1 − P(toffee) = 1 − 0.3 = 0.7
>
> - How to find all the possible outcomes when two events are combined.
>   By **listing** the outcomes systematically.
>   By using a **possibility space diagram**.

Exercise 40

1 Here are three possible events:

    A A coin when tossed will come down heads.
    B It will snow in August in London.
    C There will be a baby born tomorrow.

Which of the three events is
(a) most likely to happen,
(b) least likely to happen? *Edexcel*

2 Copy the probability line.

(a) Mark with *H* the probability of getting a head when a fair coin is thrown.
(b) Mark with *S* the probability of getting a 7 when a fair six-sided dice is thrown.
(c) Mark with *N* the probability of getting a number less than 10 when a fair six-sided dice is thrown. *Edexcel*

3 A packet contains 1 red balloon, 3 white balloons and 4 blue balloons.
A balloon is taken from the packet at random.
What is the probability that it is
(a) red, (b) red or white, (c) not white?

4 A red dice and a blue dice are both numbered 1 to 6.
In a game, both dice are thrown and the total score is found by adding the two numbers.
(a) Copy the table and list all the possible ways in which to score a **total** of 6.

Ways to score a total of 6.	
Number on red dice	**Number on blue dice**

(b) Explain which is more likely, a total score of 6 or a total score of 12. *Edexcel*

5 A letter has a first-class stamp on it.
The probability that the letter will be delivered on the next working day is 0.86.
What is the probability that the letter will **not** be delivered on the next working day? *Edexcel*

6 Aimee, Georgina, Hannah and Louisa are the only runners in a race.
The probabilities of Aimee, Georgina, Hannah and Louisa winning the race are shown in the table.

Aimee	Georgina	Hannah	Louisa
0.3	0.2	0.4	

(a) Work out the probability that Louisa will win the race.
(b) Work out the probability that either Aimee or Hannah will win the race.

7 60 British students each visited one foreign country last week.
The two-way table shows some information about these students.

	France	Germany	Spain	Total
Female			9	34
Male	15			
Total		25	18	60

(a) Copy and complete the two-way table.

One of these students is picked at random.
(b) Write down the probability that the student visited Germany last week.

Edexcel

8 Two fair spinners are used in a game.
The first spinner is labelled   1, 1, 2, 3.
The second spinner is labelled   2, 3, 4, 5.

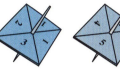

Second spinner

	2	3	4	5
1	1	2	3	4
1	1			
2	0			
3	1			

First spinner

Both spinners are spun.
The **score** is the positive difference between the numbers shown.

(a) Copy and complete the table to show the possible scores.
(b) What is the most likely score?
(c) Work out the probability of getting a score of 1.

Edexcel

9 The letters of the word   A B B E Y   are written on separate cards and placed in a box.
A card is taken from the box at random.

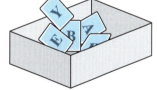

(a) What is the probability that it is the letter B?
(b) The probability that it is a vowel is 0.4.
What is the probability that it is not a vowel?

10 Petra has 5 numbered cards.
She uses the cards to do this experiment:

> Shuffle the cards and then record the number on the top card.

She repeats the experiment 20 times and gets these results.

3   3   2   3   4   3   5   2   3   4
3   5   3   3   4   2   5   3   4   2

(a) What is the relative frequency of getting a 3?
(b) What numbers do you think are on the five cards?
Give a reason for your answer.
(c) She repeats the experiment 500 times.
Estimate the number of times she will get a 5.
Give a reason for your answer.

11 Jeff tosses a coin three times.
(a) List all the possible outcomes.
(b) What is the probability that he gets one head and two tails?

12 A bag contains counters which are green, blue or white.
When one counter is picked at random,
the probability that it will be green is $\frac{1}{2}$,   the probability that it will be blue is $\frac{1}{8}$.
(a) What is the probability that a counter picked out at random will be either green or blue?
(b) What is the probability that a counter picked out at random will be either white or green?

Edexcel

Handling Data
Non-calculator Paper

Do not use a calculator for this exercise.

1 The pictogram shows the number of videos hired from a shop each day last week.

On Monday 6 videos were hired.

(a) How many videos does ⬭⬭ represent?

(b) How many videos were hired on Thursday?

70 videos were hired altogether last week.

(c) How many videos were hired on Saturday?

2 Here is a spinner.
The spinner is spun.

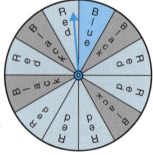

(a) (i) Which colour is least likely?
  (ii) Give a reason for your answer.

(b) Copy the probability line and mark with an *X* the probability that the colour will be Red.

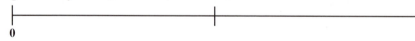

(c) Write down the probability that the colour will be Blue.

Edexcel

3 The results of a survey of the holiday destinations of people booking holidays abroad are shown in the bar chart.

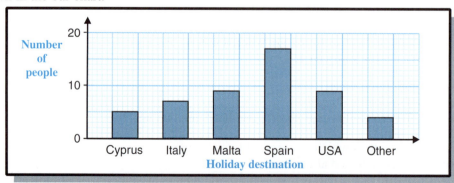

(a) Which holiday destination is the mode?
(b) How many more people are going to Spain than to Cyprus?
(c) How many people are included in the survey?

4. Here are nine numbers.

   7 3 4 9 3 9 3 3 4

   Find (a) the mode, (b) the median, (c) the range, (d) the mean.   Edexcel

5. The graph shows the distribution of the best height jumped by each girl in a high jump competition.

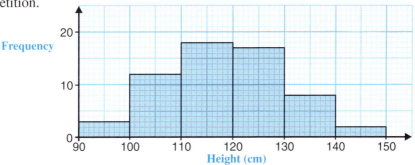

   (a) How many girls jumped less than 100 cm?
   (b) How many girls jumped between 100 cm and 120 cm?
   (c) How many girls took part in the competition?

6. Sylvester did a survey to find the most popular pantomime.
   (a) The results for children are shown in the table.

Pantomime	Aladdin	Cinderella	Jack and the Bean Stalk	Peter Pan
Number of children	45	35	25	15

   (i) Draw a clearly labelled pie chart to illustrate this information.
   (ii) Which pantomime is the mode?

   (b) The results for adults are shown in the pie chart.
   (i) 20 adults chose Aladdin.
   How many adults were included in the survey?
   (ii) What percentage of adults chose Cinderella?

7. A game is played with two spinners.
   You multiply the two numbers on which the spinners land to get the score.

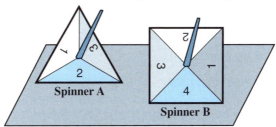

   This score is: 2 × 4 = 8

   (a) Copy and complete the table to show all the possible scores. One has been done for you.

×	1	2	3	4
1				
2				8
3				

   (b) Work out the probability of getting a score of 6.
   (c) Work out the probability of getting a score that is an odd number.   Edexcel

8 The names and prices of four second-hand cars are shown in the table.

Name	Nippy sports	Tuff hatchback	Ace supermini	Mega estate
Price	£12 000	£4000	£6000	£18 000

On the scatter graph, each letter represents one of the cars.

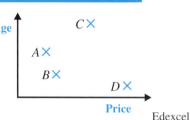

(a) Use the information shown in the table and in the scatter graph to write down the letter which represents each car.

(b) Write down the name of the oldest car.

Edexcel

9 The mean of four numbers is 7.
The mean of six different numbers is 8.
Calculate the mean of all ten numbers.

10 Linzi is doing a survey to find if there should be a supermarket in her neighbourhood.
This is one of her questions.

> "Do you agree that having a supermarket in the neighbourhood would make it easier for you to do your shopping and if we did have one would you use it?"

Give two reasons why this question is unsuitable in its present form.

11 The lengths of 20 bolts, in centimetres, is shown.

7.4 5.8 4.5 5.0 6.5 6.6 7.0 5.4 4.8 6.4
5.4 6.2 7.2 5.5 4.8 6.5 5.0 6.0 6.5 6.8

(a) Draw a stem and leaf diagram to show this information.
(b) What is the range in the lengths of these bolts?

12 The table shows information about a group of students.

	Can speak French	Cannot speak French
Male	5	20
Female	12	38

(a) One of these students is chosen at random.
What is the probability that the student can speak French?

(b) Pru says,

> "If a female student is chosen at random she is more likely to be able to speak French than if a male student is chosen at random."

Is she correct? Explain your answer.

13 Some people were asked how many National Lottery tickets they bought last week.
The results are shown in the table.

Number of tickets	0	1	2	3	4	5	6
Number of people	2	7	5	2	0	3	1

(a) Which number of tickets is the mode?
(b) Work out the median number of tickets.
(c) Find the mean number of tickets.

Edexcel

14 A bag contains 50 cubes of which 7 are red.
A cube is taken from the bag at random.
(a) The probability that it is white is 0.3.
What is the probability that it is not white?
(b) What is the probability that it is either white or red?

Handling Data Calculator Paper

You may use a calculator for this exercise.

1 The table shows the number of books borrowed from a library during five days.

Day	Monday	Tuesday	Wednesday	Thursday	Friday
Number of books	40	35	30	15	50

(a) How many books were borrowed during these five days?
(b) Draw a pictogram to represent the information. Use 📖 to represent 10 books.

2 Sarah watched a water ride at a theme park.
She counted the number of people in each of 20 boats. These numbers are shown below.

2 3 1 2 2 3 4 5 4 1
1 2 2 3 2 4 5 4 2 4

(a) Copy and complete the frequency table.

Number of people in boat	Tally	Frequency
1		
2		

(b) Write down the mode of the number of people in a boat.

Emily asked 5 people the number of rides each of them had been on.
The numbers are shown below.
6 8 7 6 10

(c) Work out the mean number of rides per person.

Edexcel

3 The graph shows the results of a traffic survey outside Ashurst School.
The number of each type of vehicle is shown as a percentage of the total number of vehicles seen on the day of the survey.

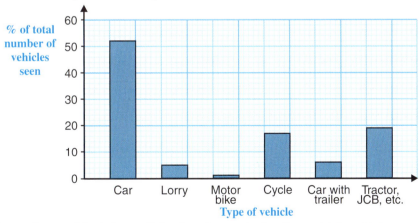

Joe walks outside Ashurst School and records the first vehicle which passes.
(a) Write **TRUE** or **FALSE** for each of these statements.
  (i) The vehicle is **most likely** to be a car.
  (ii) The vehicle is **likely** to be a motorbike.
  (iii) The vehicle is **unlikely** to be a lorry.

Errol, from Ashurst School, said, "You would get very similar results outside **any** school."
(b) Explain briefly how you could test whether this statement is true.

Edexcel

4 A company makes hearing aids.
A hearing aid is chosen at random. The probability that it has a fault is 0.09.
Work out the probability that a hearing aid, chosen at random, will **not** have a fault. *Edexcel*

5 Karen is playing a game with these cards.
One card is taken at random from the letters.
One card is taken at random from the numbers.
(a) List all the possible outcomes.
(b) What is the probability of getting an **X** or a **2**?

6 Mark throws a fair coin. He gets a head.
Mark's sister then throws the same coin.
(a) What is the probability that she will get a head?

Mark throws the coin 30 times.
(b) Explain why he may not get exactly 15 heads and 15 tails. *Edexcel*

7 The table shows the number of peas in a sample of pods.

Number of peas	1	2	3	4	5	6	7	8
Number of pods	0	0	2	3	5	7	2	1

(a) How many pods were in the sample?
(b) What is the modal number of peas in a pod?
(c) What is the range in the number of peas in a pod?
(d) Draw a bar chart to show this information.

8 The stem and leaf diagram shows the weights, in grams, of letters posted by a secretary.

```
        1 | 5  means 15 grams
    1 | 5  8
    2 | 0  4  5  6  8  8
    3 | 1  2  3  5  7
    4 | 2  5
```

(a) How many letters were posted?
(b) What is the median weight of one of these letters?
(c) What is the range in the weights of these letters?
(d) Calculate the mean weight of a letter.

9 A railway company wanted to show the improvements in its train service over 3 years. This graph was drawn.

Explain why this graph may be misleading.

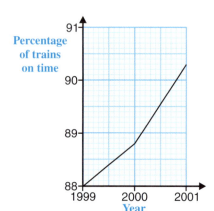

Edexcel

10 A box contains 20 plastic ducks.
3 of the ducks are green, 10 are blue and the rest are yellow.
A duck is taken from the box at random.
What is the probability that it is (a) green, (b) yellow?

11 Siân wants to collect information about the different ways in which students travel to school.
Design a suitable data collection sheet that Siân could use to collect the information. *Edexcel*

12 Bhavana asked some people which region their favourite football team came from.
The table shows her results.

Region	Midlands	London	Southern England	Northern England
Frequency	22	36	8	24

Complete an accurate pie chart to show these results. *Edexcel*

13 Ten men took part in a long jump competition.
The table shows the heights of the ten men and the best jumps they made.

Best jump (m)	5.33	6.00	5.00	5.95	4.80	5.72	4.60	5.80	4.40	5.04
Height of men (m)	1.70	1.80	1.65	1.75	1.65	1.74	1.60	1.75	1.60	1.67

(a) Plot the points as a scatter graph.
(b) Describe the relationship between the heights of the men and the best jumps they made.
(c) Draw a line of best fit.
(d) Use your line of best fit to estimate
  (i) the height of a man who could make a best jump of 5.2 m,
  (ii) the best jump of a man of height 1.73 m. *Edexcel*

14 A youth club has 60 members.
40 of the members are boys. 20 of the members are girls.
The mean number of videos watched last week by all 60 members was 2.8.
The mean number of videos watched last week by the 40 boys was 3.3.
Calculate the mean number of videos watched last week by the 20 girls. *Edexcel*

15 Grace and Gemma were carrying out a survey on the food people eat in the school canteen.
Grace wrote the question: **"Which foods do you eat?"**
Gemma said that this question was too vague.
Write down two ways in which this question could be improved. *Edexcel*

16 Jason grows potatoes. He weighed 100 potatoes and recorded the weights to the nearest gram.
The table shows information about the weights (w) of the 100 potatoes.

Weight (w grams)	Frequency
$0 \leq w < 20$	0
$20 \leq w < 40$	18
$40 \leq w < 60$	28
$60 \leq w < 80$	25
$80 \leq w < 100$	19
$100 \leq w < 120$	10

(a) Draw a frequency polygon to show this information.
(b) Work out an estimate for the mean weight of these potatoes.
(c) Find the class interval that contains the median. *Edexcel*

17 Tony throws a biased dice 100 times. The table shows his results.

Score	1	2	3	4	5	6
Frequency	12	13	17	10	18	30

He throws the dice once more.
(a) Find an estimate for the probability that he will get a 6.

Emma has a biased coin. The probability that the biased coin will land on a head is 0.7.
Emma is going to throw the coin 250 times.
(b) Work out an estimate for the number of times the coin will land on a head. *Edexcel*

Non-calculator Paper

Do not use a calculator for this exercise.

1 (a) Write the number 6740 in words.
(b) Write the value of the 7 in the number 6740.
Edexcel

2 The table shows the number of cars parked in an office car park each day.

Day	Monday	Tuesday	Wednesday	Thursday	Friday
Number of cars	8	12	6	9	10

(a) How many more cars were parked on Tuesday than on Thursday?
(b) Draw a pictogram to represent the information. Use ⊕ to represent 4 cars.

3 (a) Put these numbers in order of size, smallest first.

$$105 \quad 30 \quad 7 \quad 19 \quad 2002$$

(b) Work out. (i) $105 - 30$ (ii) 19×7 (iii) $2002 \div 7$

4 Stephen and Edward are playing a game. One player has to describe a sequence of numbers. Then the other player has to write down the first four numbers in the sequence.

Stephen says, "My sequence starts with 2. To get the next number you have to add 5 to the previous number."
(a) What are the next three numbers Edward should write?

When it is his turn, Edward says, "My sequence starts with 100. To get the next number you have to take away 9 from the previous number."
(b) What are the next three numbers Stephen should write?
Edexcel

5 Use these numbers to answer the following questions. $\quad 3 \quad 4 \quad 13 \quad 27 \quad 35 \quad 64$

(a) Which number is (i) a factor of 16, (ii) a multiple of 9, (iii) a square number?
(b) Which two numbers add up to 40?

6 (a) Copy and shade $\frac{2}{3}$ of this shape.
(b) Write $\frac{3}{5}$ (i) as a decimal,
(ii) as a percentage.
(c) (i) Write down **thirty-one thousand three hundred and two** in figures.
(ii) Write down 13 820 to the nearest thousand.
(d) Explain how you would estimate 97×62.
Edexcel

7 Helen is standing at *H*. She is facing North. She turns anticlockwise through 1 right angle.
(a) In what direction is she now facing?

Later Harry stands at *H*. He faces South.
He turns clockwise through $1\frac{1}{2}$ right angles.
(b) In what direction will he then be facing?

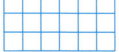

Edexcel

8 (a) A roll costs *d* pence. How much will 5 rolls cost?
(b) A cake costs 25 pence more than a roll. How much does a cake cost?

9 (a) On graph paper plot the points $P(4, 1)$ and $Q(2, -5)$.
(b) Find the coordinates of the midpoint of the line segment *PQ*.

10 Use the formula $P = 5m + 2n$ to find the value of *P* when $m = 4$ and $n = 3$.

⑪ The diagram shows a rectangle and a triangle drawn on 1 cm squared paper.
(a) How many lines of symmetry has
(i) the rectangle,
(ii) the triangle?
(b) What is the perimeter of the rectangle?
(c) What is the area of the triangle?

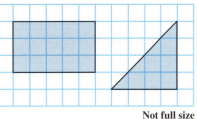

Not full size

⑫ Sports Wear Ltd. hire out ski-suits. The cost of hiring a ski-suit is calculated using this rule.

> Four pounds per day plus a fixed charge of five pounds.

(a) How much would it cost to hire a ski-suit for 8 days?
(b) Heather paid £65 to hire a ski-suit. For how many days did she hire it?

⑬ This is a conversion graph for miles and kilometres.
(a) How many miles are equivalent to 32 kilometres?
(b) How many kilometres are equivalent to 15 miles?

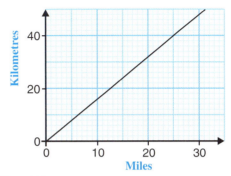

Edexcel

⑭ Work out. (a) 563 × 78 (b) 793 ÷ 26

Edexcel

⑮ Here are the numbers of people living in the different houses in a short road.

4, 2, 3, 4, 5, 1, 3, 2

(a) Work out the mean number of people per house.
(b) Work out the range of the number of people living in a house.

One of the houses is to be chosen at random.
(c) Draw a probability line and mark with the letter X the probability that the house chosen will be the one with 5 people.

Edexcel

⑯ Write down the order of rotational symmetry for these shapes.

A   B C

Edexcel

⑰ At midday the temperature in Moscow was −6°C.
At midday the temperature in Norwich was 4°C.
(a) How many degrees higher was the temperature in Norwich than the temperature in Moscow?

At midnight the temperature in Norwich had fallen by 7 degrees from 4°C.
(b) Work out the midnight temperature in Norwich.

Edexcel

⑱ Shreena has a bag of 20 sweets.
10 of the sweets are red. 3 of the sweets are black. The rest of the sweets are white.
Shreena chooses one sweet at random.
What is the probability that Shreena will choose (a) a red sweet, (b) a white sweet?

Edexcel

⑲ The time it takes to cook a turkey can be found using this rule.

Allow 40 minutes per kilogram *plus* an extra 20 minutes.

A turkey weighing 4.5 kg is placed in the oven at 9.45 am. At what time will it be cooked?
Give your answer in 12-hour clock time.

20 In the diagram *PQ* and *RS* are straight lines.

(a) (i) Work out the value of *a*.
(ii) Give a reason for your answer.
(b) (i) Work out the value of *b*.
(ii) Give a reason for your answer.
(c) (i) Work out the value of *c*.
(ii) Give a reason for your answer.

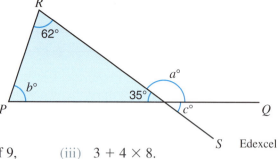

Edexcel

21 (a) Work out (i) $7 - 3.72$, (ii) $\frac{3}{5}$ of 9, (iii) $3 + 4 \times 8$.
(b) What is the value of $5^2 + \sqrt{36}$?

22 (a) Simplify. (i) $a + 2a + 4a$ (ii) $2x + 5y - 3x + 6y$ (iii) $a \times a \times 3$
(b) Solve. (i) $5x = 15$ (ii) $3x - 2 = 10$ (iii) $2x + 1 = 7$
(c) Find the value of $3x + y^3$ when $x = -1$ and $y = 2$.

23 In a survey, people going to France were asked:
Where will you be staying on holiday?
The pie chart shows the results.
(a) What percentage were camping?
(b) 35 people were staying in a caravan.
How many people took part in the survey?

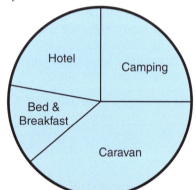

24 Seth takes $2\frac{1}{2}$ hours to travel 150 km.
Calculate his average speed for the journey.

25 (a) Write $\frac{7}{9}$ as a decimal. Give your answer correct to two decimal places.
(b) Write 33%, 0.3, $\frac{8}{25}$ and $\frac{1}{3}$ in order of size, smallest first.
(c) Work out: (i) $\frac{7}{9} + \frac{1}{3}$ (ii) $\frac{3}{5} \div 4$. Give your answers as fractions.

26 To calculate the number of mince pies, *m*, to make for a Christmas Party for *p* people, Donna uses the formula $m = 2p + 10$.
(a) How many mince pies would she make for a party of 12 people?
(b) Donna makes 60 mince pies for another party.
How many people are expected at this party?

27 Sixty teenagers take part in a dancing competition. The ratio of males to females is 1 : 5.
(a) How many males take part?

After the first round 6 males and 26 females are knocked out.
(b) What is the ratio of males to females left in the competition?
Give your answer in its simplest form.

28 A bag of Estima potatoes weighs 10 kg and costs £2.60.
(a) Estimate the weight of the potatoes in pounds.
(b) King Edward potatoes cost 15% more than Estima potatoes.
What is the cost of a 10 kg bag of King Edward potatoes?

29 (a) Draw and label the lines $y = x + 1$ and $x + y = 3$ for values of *x* from -1 to 3.
(b) Write down the coordinates of the point where the lines cross.

30 The numbers on these cards are coded. The sum of the numbers on these 3 cards is 41.

| *x* | $2x - 1$ | $3x$ |

(a) Form an equation in *x*.
(b) By solving your equation, find the numbers on the cards.

31 $32 \times 129 = 4128$
Write down the value of (a) 3.2×1.29, (b) $0.32 \times 129\,000$. *Edexcel*

32 A farmer has two crop circles in his field.
One circle has a radius of 9 m and the other has a diameter of 12 m.
Calculate, in terms of π, the circumference of the smaller circle.

33 Solve the equations. (a) $11x + 5 = x + 25$ (b) $3(4y - 9) = 81$ *Edexcel*

34 (a) Write as a product of its prime factors (i) 48, (ii) 108.
(b) Hence, find the least common multiple of 48 and 108.

35 A concrete block weighs 11 kg, correct to the nearest kilogram.
Write down the greatest and least possible weight of the block.

36 A sequence begins: 2, 5, 8, 11, ...
Write in terms of n, the nth term of the sequence.

37 The diagram shows the positions of shapes P, Q and R.

(a) Describe fully the single transformation which takes P onto Q.

(b) Describe fully the single transformation which takes P onto R.

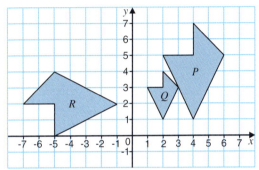

38 The table shows information about the number of fillings the students in a class had last year.

Number of students	0	1	2	3	More than 3
Number of fillings	10	5	4	2	1

The headteacher is to choose a student at random from the class.
Find the probability that she will choose a student who had
(a) exactly 1 filling, (b) 2 or more fillings, (c) either 1 filling or 2 fillings. *Edexcel*

39 (a) Copy and complete the table of values for $y = x^2 - 3x + 1$.

x	-1	0	1	2	3	4
y		1	-1			5

(b) Draw the graph of $y = x^2 - 3x + 1$ for values of x from -1 to 4.
(c) Use your graph to find the value of y when $x = 1.5$.
(d) Use your graph to solve the equation $x^2 - 3x + 1 = 0$.

40 Cocoa is sold in cylindrical tins. The height of a tin is 7.9 cm. The radius of a tin is 4.1 cm.
Use approximations to estimate the volume of a tin. Show all your working.

41 (a) Factorise. (i) $5a - 10$ (ii) $x^2 - 6x$
(b) Expand and simplify. (i) $3(a + 4) - 5(2 - a)$ (ii) $(x - 2)(x - 4)$
(c) Make t the subject of the formula. $W = 5t + 3$
(d) Simplify. $m^2 \times m^3$

42 These formulae represent quantities connected with containers, where a, b and c are dimensions. $2(ab + bc + cd)$ abc $\sqrt{a^2 + b^2}$ $4(a + b + c)$
Which of these formulae represent lengths? Explain how you know.

43 Solve the inequality $1 < 2x + 3 \leq 7$ and show the solution on a number line.

Calculator Paper

You may use a calculator for this exercise.

1 (a) Which of the numbers 8, −4, 0 or 5 is an odd number?
  (b) Write the number 3568 to the nearest 10.
  (c) What is the value of the 4 in the number 3.42?

2 (a) List these numbers in order, smallest first.

  13   5   −7   0   −1

  (b) What is the difference between the largest number and the smallest number in your list?

3 Copy the diagram and draw a reflection of the shape in the mirror line *PQ*.

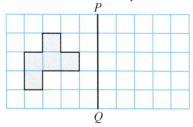

4 Farah buys 2 pens at 84p each, 3 folders at £1.35 each, 1 pencil case at £1.49.
She pays with a £10 note.
Work out how much change Farah should get from £10.

Edexcel

5 Here are some patterns made out of matchsticks.

        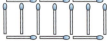

Pattern number 1   Pattern number 2   Pattern number 3

  (a) Draw a diagram of Pattern number 4.
  (b) Copy and complete the table to show the number of matchsticks needed for Pattern number 4 and Pattern number 5.

Pattern number	1	2	3	4	5
Number of matchsticks	5	9	13		

  (c) Work out the pattern number that needs exactly 41 matchsticks.
  (d) (i) How many matchsticks are needed for Pattern number 100?
    (ii) Describe how you found this answer.

Edexcel

6 Natasha uses this formula to work out her Total pay.

  Total pay = Rate per hour × Number of hours + Bonus

Her Rate per hour is £5.50.   She works for 35 hours.   She has a Bonus of £12.50.
Work out her Total pay.

Edexcel

7 (a) What metric unit of length would you use to measure the length of a large coach?

  (b) Using the unit you gave in part (a), estimate the length of a large coach.

Edexcel

8 On a musical keyboard there are 5 black keys for every 7 white keys.
The keyboard has 28 white keys.
How many black keys does it have?

9 Which of these triangles are congruent?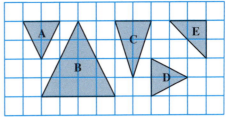

10 Tom Brown was going to America for his holiday.
The bank sold him £450 worth of dollars at a rate of 1.52 dollars to the pound.
How many dollars did Tom receive?   *Edexcel*

11 The times of rail journeys from Guildford to Waterloo are shown.

Guildford	0703	0722	0730	0733	0749	0752
Worplesdon	0708	0727	—	0739	—	0757
Clapham Junction	0752	—	0800	0822	—	—
Waterloo	0800	0815	0808	0830	0823	0844

(a) Karen catches the 0722 from Guildford to Waterloo.
How many minutes does the journey take?
(b) Graham arrives at Worplesdon station at 0715.
What is the time of the next train to Clapham Junction?

12 The diagram shows two gear wheels.
The large wheel has 24 teeth. The small wheel has 12 teeth.
Describe what happens to the small wheel when the large wheel
is turned through 90° in a clockwise direction.

13 Solve (a) $3x = 18$,   (b) $3x - 1 = 8$.

14 Mary's floor is a rectangle 8 m long and 5 m wide.
She wants to cover the floor completely with carpet tiles.
Each carpet tile is square with sides of length 50 cm. Each carpet tile costs £4.19.
Work out the cost of covering Mary's floor completely with carpet tiles.   *Edexcel*

15 Here is an Input-Output diagram.

(a) What is the Output when the Input is −1?
(b) What is the Input when the Output is 9?
(c) When the Input is x, what is the Output in terms of x?

16 Cheri is paid a basic rate of £6.40 per hour for a 35-hour week.
Overtime is paid at $1\frac{1}{2}$ times the basic rate.
Last week she worked 41 hours. Calculate her pay for last week.

17 Work out the value of $\dfrac{5.4 - 6.3^2}{0.3}$.   *Edexcel*

18 A fairground ride is decorated with 240 coloured lights.
(a) 15% of the lights are red. How many red lights are there?
(b) 30 of the 240 lights are not working. What percentage of lights are not working?

19 Write these numbers in order of size. Start with the smallest number. $\frac{7}{8}$, 80%, 0.9, $\frac{8}{9}$.   *Edexcel*

20 $P = x^2 - 5x$. Find the value of P when $x = -4$.   *Edexcel*

21 A rowing boat has 8 oarsmen and a cox. The mean weight of the oarsmen is 73.2 kg.
When the cox is included the mean weight is 71.6 kg. Calculate the weight of the cox.

22 The diagrams show a quadrilateral, a regular hexagon and a regular octagon.
Work out the size of the angles marked $a°$, $b°$ and $c°$.

 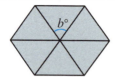 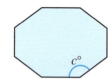

Not drawn accurately

Edexcel

23 (a) A dinner plate has a diameter of 18 cm. Calculate the circumference of the dinner plate.
(b) A tea plate has a radius of 8 cm. Calculate the area of the tea plate.

24 Work out $\frac{2}{5} - \frac{1}{3}$, giving your answer as a fraction.

25 This rule is used to find out how far apart to plant two bushes.

> Add the heights of the bushes.   Divide your answer by 3.

Ben is going to plant two different bushes.
He should plant them 50 cm apart.
The height of one of the bushes is 90 cm.
(a) Work out the height of the other bush.

The heights of two different bushes are a cm and b cm.
The two bushes should be planted d cm apart.
(b) Write down a formula for d in terms of a and b.

Edexcel

26 (a) Simplify (i) $4x + 7y + 2x - 3y$,   (ii) $2pq + pq$.
(b) Factorise $3t - 12$.

Edexcel

27 Bob cycles from home to work.
The travel graph shows his journey.

(a) On his way to work Bob stopped to buy a newspaper.
At what time did he stop?

(b) (i) During which part of his journey did Bob cycle fastest?
Give a reason for your answer.
(ii) Calculate his average speed in kilometres per hour for this part of his journey.

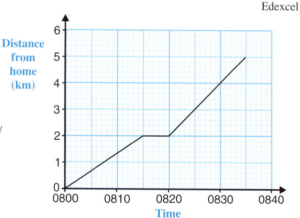

28 The table shows the birth rate and the life expectancy for 12 countries.

Birth rate	13	17	21	25	28	30	31	34	38	41	44	47
Life expectancy (years)	75	73	71	68	65	62	61	65	61	56	51	49

(a) Plot the information as a scatter graph.
(b) Describe the relationship between the birth rate and the life expectancy.
(c) Draw a line of best fit on your scatter graph.

The birth rate in a country is 42.
(d) Use your scatter graph to estimate the life expectancy in that country.

Edexcel

29 The perimeter of the pentagon is 200 cm.
Work out the value of x.

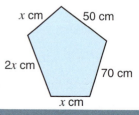

Edexcel

118

30 John has a spinner in the shape of a regular pentagon.
Scores of 1, 2, 3, 4, 5 are equally likely when the spinner is spun.
John spins the spinner 200 times and records the scores.
Approximately how many times will he score an even number?

Edexcel

31 A hang glider flies 2.8 km on a bearing of 070° from P to Q and then 2 km on a bearing of 200° from Q to R.
(a) Make a scale drawing to show the flight of the hang glider from P to Q to R.
Use a scale of 1 cm to 200 m.
(b) From R the hang glider flies directly back to P.
Use your drawing to find the distance and bearing of P from R.

32 Solve the equations. (a) $3y + 7 = 28$ (b) $2(3p + 2) = 19$ (c) $3t - 4 = 5t - 10$

Edexcel

33 The diagram shows a prism. The cross-section of the prism is a trapezium.
The lengths of the parallel sides of the trapezium are 8 cm and 6 cm.
The distance between the parallel sides of the trapezium is 5 cm.
The length of the prism is 20 cm.
(a) Work out the volume of the prism.

The prism is made out of gold.
Gold has a density of 19.3 grams per cm³.
(b) Work out the mass of the prism.
Give your answer in kilograms.

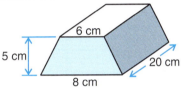

Edexcel

34 Use a trial and improvement method to find a solution to the equation $x^3 + x = 57$.
Show all your working and give your answer correct to one decimal place.

35 Some students took part in a sponsored silence.
The frequency diagram shows the distribution of their times.

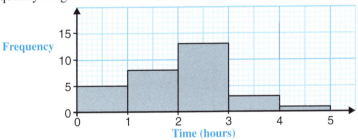

(a) How many students took part?
(b) Which time interval contains the median of their times?
(c) Calculate an estimate of the mean of their times.

36 Bill gave his three daughters a total of £32.40.
The money was shared in the ratios 4 : 3 : 2.
Jane had the largest share.
Work out how much money Bill gave to Jane.

Edexcel

37 The diagram shows a semi-circle with diameter AB.
C is a point on the circumference.
$\angle ACB = 90°$.
$AC = 6$ cm and $CB = 8$ cm.

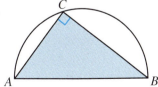

Calculate the area of the shaded triangle as a percentage of the area of the semi-circle.

38 Use your calculator to find the value of $\dfrac{29.7 + 17.3}{1.54 \times 68.5}$.
Give your answer to a suitable degree of accuracy **and** give a reason for your choice.

Answers

SECTION 1

Exercise 1 — Page 1

1. (a) **350 000**
   (b) (i) Twenty-five thousand four hundred
       (ii) 5 thousands, 5000
2. 117, 100, 85, 23, 9
3. (a) 8 or 14   (b) 11, 14   (c) 8 and 15
4. (a) 40   (b) 150 000
5. Sixty million
6. 93 pence
7. (a) 81   (b) (i) 35   (ii) 100   (iii) 10
8. (a) 1005   (b) 191   (c) 183
9.

	100 g	200 g	300 g	Total
Ground	15	50	55	120
Powder	80	35	26	141
Granules	40	45	54	139
Total	135	130	135	400

10. (a) (i) 2358   (ii) 8523
    (b) 500   (c) 50   (d) 6165
11. (a) 12 000   (b) 500   (c) 175   (d) 15
12. (a) (i) 6   (ii) 80   (iii) 200 000
    (b) 6
13. 32 pence
14. (a) 158 km   (b) 163 km
    (c) **Manchester** and **Liverpool**
15. £181 per month
16. £10.68
17. 50 boxes
18. (a) 18   (b) 12   (c) 3
19. 70 kg
20. 115 cm
21. 33 069
22. £6894
23. 218 days
24. (a) 1620 hamsters   (b) 65 cages
25. (a) $1 + 2 + 3 + 4 = \frac{4 \times 5}{2} = 10$
    (b) 5050

SECTION 2

Exercise 2 — Page 3

1. 0.065 and 0.9
2. 1.08, 1.118, 1.18, 1.80
3. (a) 18.59   (b) 11.37   (c) 2.9   (d) 2.64
4. 4.9 kg
5. £26.97
6. £1.69
7. (a) 320   (b) 0.32
8. (a) 560. E.g. divide by 10, multiply by 8.
   (b) 150. E.g. multiply by 10, divide by 4.
9. 1.57 m
10. (a) There are two figures after the decimal points in the question but only one in the answer.
    (b) (i) 0.12   (ii) 0.06
11. (a) (i) 4.02   (ii) 12
    (b) (i) 136   (ii) 0.245
12. (a) 7.36   (b) 3.2   (c) 230
13. 32 pence
14. (a) $\frac{3}{10}$ (b) $\frac{3}{100}$ (c) $\frac{33}{100}$
15. 40 minutes
16. $0 < m < 1$. E.g. $\frac{1}{2}, \frac{2}{5}$
17. 11.5 p/kg.   Bag: 38 p/kg,   sack: 26.5 p/kg.
18. £3.61
19. 403 km
20. 17.76792453

SECTION 3

Exercise 3 — Page 6

1. (a) 626   (b) 630   (c) 600
2. 8700
3. 19 500
4. 300 km + 100 km = 400 km
5. (a) 9000, 1300, 1700
   (b) $\frac{9000}{1300 + 1700} = \frac{9000}{3000} = 3$
6. $\frac{3000 \times 40}{100} = £1200$
7. (a) $15 \div 3$ (b) 5 pairs
8. (a) 40×90 (b) 3600   (c) 49
9. (a) $2000 \div 40 = 50$ (b) 50
10. (a) 100 is bigger than 97, **and** 50 is bigger than 49.
    (b) Smaller.   1000 is smaller than 1067, **and** 50 is bigger than 48.
11. (a) $20 \times 70 = 1400$ seats
    (b) $1400 \times £10 = £14\,000$
12. (a) 635   (b) 644
13. Length of book would only be measured to nearest millimetre, i.e., 21.3 cm.
14. 49.5 m
15. 5 tickets
16. 17 boxes
17. $\frac{400 + 200}{40} = \frac{600}{40} = 15$.   Answer is wrong.
18. $\frac{70 \times 400}{200} = 140$
19. (a) 40 000   (b) 0.000 7
20. $\frac{0.3 \times 80}{5} = 4.8$ (or 5)

21. (a) $\frac{20 \times 60}{100} = \frac{1200}{100} = 12$
    (b) $12 - 10.875 = 1.125$
22. (a) $\frac{9000}{10} \times 90\text{p} = £810$
    (b) 9000 is larger than 8873, 10 is smaller than 11, and 90 is larger than 89.9.
23. Minimum: £95, maximum: £104.99
24. (a) 14.95 (b) 15.0
25. (a) 680 (b) 700
26. No. For example, an answer of 0.01634… is 0.02 to 2 d.p. and 0.016 to 2 s.f. 0.016 is more accurate.
27. (a) 8.299 492 386 (b) 8.30
28. 0.3
29. (a) 5.98 to 2 d.p. (b) $\frac{90 \times 4}{70 - 10} = \frac{360}{60} = 6$

SECTION 4

Exercise 4 — Page 8

1. (a) $-3°C$ (b) $-13°C$
2. (a) Oslo (b) Warsaw
3. 140 m
4. $-9, -3, 0, 5, 7, 17$
5. (a) 5 (b) -15
   (c) -50 (d) -2
6. (a) Montreal (b) $45°C$
7. £57 overdrawn $(-£57)$
8. (a) 6 degrees (b) Between 1200 and 1800
9. (a) (i) $7°C$ (ii) $6°C$
   (b) $2°C$ (c) $-15°C$
10. (a) 4 (b) 11 (c) -3
11. 7 degrees
12. (a) -4 (b) -8
13. (a) (i) -20 (ii) 21
    (b) (i) -4 (ii) 3
14. $20°F$
15. (a) -20 (b) -15
16. 5

SECTION 5

Exercise 5 — Page 10

1. (a) $\frac{2}{5}$
   (b) Shade 4 parts.
2. $\frac{3}{9}$ and $\frac{7}{35}$
3. (a) $\frac{7}{10}$ as $\frac{4}{5} = \frac{8}{10}$
   (b) E.g. $\frac{5}{12}$
4. $\frac{7}{12}, \frac{2}{3}, \frac{5}{6}$
5. £8
6. 15 miles
7. 8
8. $\frac{5}{12}$
9. £46
10. £3.14
11. £104
12. $\frac{1}{5}$
13. (a) $\frac{11}{18}$ (b) $\frac{3}{56}$
14. (a) 0.167 (b) 1.7, 1.67, 1.66, $1\frac{1}{6}$, 1.067
15. (a) $\frac{1}{6}$ (b) $1\frac{1}{8}$
16. $\frac{7}{24}$
17. $\frac{5}{9}$
18. $\frac{9}{20}$
19. £3.80 per kilogram

SECTION 6

Exercise 6 — Page 13

1. (a) 12, 20, 24, 30, 100
   (b) 20, 30, 100 (c) 24 is double 12
2. (a) 1, 2, 3, 6, 9, 18 (b) 35
   (c) 9 has more than 2 factors: 1, 3, 9
3. (a) 25 (b) 8
4. (a) 36 (b) 10
5. No. $2^2 + 3^2 = 4 + 9 = 13$
   $(2 + 3)^2 = 5^2 = 25$
6. 23
7. 1, 2, 3, 6
8. (a) 5 (b) 64
9. (a) 55 (b) 8100 (c) 200
10. No. $1^3 + 2^3 = 1 + 8 = 9$
    $3^3 = 27$
11. (a) 72 (b) 17 (c) 112
12. 30
13. (a) $2^2 \times 3^2$ (b) $3^2 \times 5$
    (c) 9 (d) 180
14. 36
15. 30 seconds
16. (a) 5 (b) 0.25
    (c) $\sqrt{225}$. $\sqrt{225} = 15$, $2^4 = 16$
17. (a) $x = 9$ (b) $x = 3$
18. (a) 3^5 (b) 5^3 (c) 2^2
19. (a) 2 500 000 (b) 0.000 037
20. 1.25
21. (a) 8 and 9 (b) 8.37
22. (a) 0.14 (b) 175.616
23. 45.02
24. (a) 18.277415… (b) 18.28
25. (a) 46.416376… (b) 46
26. 41.2
27. (a) 10.657
    (b) $\sqrt{\frac{4}{0.2^2}} = \sqrt{\frac{4}{0.04}} = \sqrt{100} = 10$

SECTION 7

Exercise 7 — Page 15

1. (a) 30% (b) 25% (c) 40%
2. 0.02, 20%, $\frac{1}{2}$
3. (a) 2 pence (b) 15 kg (c) £45
4. Daisy. Daisy scored $\frac{4}{5} = 80\%$.

121

5. £13.50
6. 125 people
7. 700 people
8. 60 pence
9. 360
10. 5%
11. 60%
12. (a) 126 (b) 30%
13. £72
14. £8.45 per hour
15. £9.66
16. 25%
17. 15%
18. 46%
19. 81
20. £14 000

SECTION 8

Exercise 8 — Page 17

1. (a) £7.35 (b) 9 minutes
2. (a) 0715 (b) 32 minutes (c) 0623
3. (a) 64 euros (b) £6.25
4. 12 days
5. £493.50
6. Small bar. Large: 2.66 g/p, small: 2.78 g/p
7. £75 − £73.12 = £1.88
8. £480
9. Washing Power: £247.50
   Whytes: £256.00
   Clean Up: £246.75

SECTION 9

Exercise 9 — Page 19

1. £16.25
2. £1876.25
3. £614
4. £40.74
5. 17 hours
6. £9 × 30 = £270
7. (a) £1894
   (b) £189.40
8. £5.60
9. £63.04
10. (a) (i) £12.60
       (ii) £151.20
    (b) 59 years old
11. £270.18
12. £75 per month
13. £1725.90
14. £34.91

SECTION 10

Exercise 10 — Page 21

1. (a) 1 : 3 (b) 2 : 1 (c) 2 : 3
2. 3 cm by 4 cm
3. 8 large bricks
4. 4 cm
5. 150 g butter, 120 g sugar, 135 g flour, 3 eggs, 45 ml milk.
6. (a) 70% (b) 9 women
7. 20
8. £87
9. (a) 1 : 3 (b) 20 m^3
10. £517.50
11. £44.75
12. 1 : 20 000
13. (a) £76.80 (b) £51.20

SECTION 11

Exercise 11 — Page 23

1. 64 km/h
2. $1\frac{1}{2}$ hours
3. 165 km
4. 40 minutes
5. 48 miles per hour
6. 2.5 km
7. 2 km
8. 3 km/h
9. 98 km/h
10. (a) 40 mph
    (b) 1116
11. 63.3 mph
12. 5 hours 42 minutes
13. Yes.
    $\frac{65}{80} \times 60 = 48.75$ mins
    Arrives 1029
14. 28.8 mph
15. 9.8 m/s
16. 10 m/s
17. 9 g/cm^3
18. 19 g
19. 259.3 people/km^2

Number

Non-calculator Paper — Page 25

1. (a) 45 608 (b) 46 000
2. (a) (i) 6, 10, 16, 61, 100 (ii) 193
   (b) (i) 63 (ii) 2000 (iii) 25
3. (a) 75% (b) 25%
4. (a) 16 pence (b) £1.88
5. 424 km
6. 7 hours 47 minutes
7. (a) One million (b) 3 tens, 30
8. (a) 2, 8, 12, 14, 16 (b) 3, 9, 12
   (c) 3 is the square root of 9,
       5 is the square root of 25.
9. (a) 74 pence (b) £4.90
10. £4752
11. $\frac{7}{8}$, 0.8, $\frac{3}{4}$, 70%
12. 1500 m
13. (a) 5 coaches (b) £1287.50
14. (a) 5 (b) 1, 2, 3
15. (a) 9472 (b) 25
16. £30
17. (a) 0.067, 0.56, 0.6, 0.605, 0.65
    (b) −10, −6, −4, −2, 5
    (c) $\frac{2}{5}$, $\frac{1}{2}$, $\frac{2}{3}$, $\frac{3}{4}$
18. 12 footballs
19. (a) £1.50 (b) £10.91
20. −4°C, −2°C, −1°C, 0°C, 1°C, 3°C, 7°C.
21. (a) −4 (b) 12
22. (a) 800 ÷ 20 (b) 40
23. (a) $\frac{8}{10} = \frac{4}{5}$ (b) 57.42 (c) 0.45
    (d) (i) 4.74 (ii) 0.08` (iii) 80
    (e) £23.40
24. (a) (i) 100 000 (ii) 68 (iii) 72 (iv) 0.9
    (b) 5^4, $5^4 = 625$, $4^5 = 1024$ (c) 50
25. (a) 80% (b) £125 (c) 65%

26. (a) $\frac{9}{40}$ (b) (i) $\frac{13}{20}$ (ii) $\frac{1}{6}$ (iii) $\frac{8}{15}$
    (c) $4\frac{4}{5}$ or 4.8
27. $\frac{800 \times 20}{100} = 160$
28. (a) 8100 (b) 36 000
29. (a) 34.7 (b) 400 000
30. $\frac{5}{12}$
31. $\frac{18\,000}{3500} \approx 5$, $5 \times 365 = 1825$ miles
32. (a) £42.75 (b) £34.20
33. £55.65
34. 27.5 cm
35. 59 pence
36. (a) £88.20
    (b) Cheese: 28 g, topping: 42 g
37. (a) 18 pence (b) 75%
38. £4.75
39. £1.38
40. (a) 16 km/h (b) 1106
41. (a) $\frac{31}{40}$ (b) $2\frac{11}{12}$
42. (a) 245 (b) 254
43. 264
44. 5^4
45. (a) Ruth £100, Ben £80 (b) 60%
46. (a) (i) $2^3 \times 3^2$ (ii) $2^5 \times 3$ (b) 288

Number

Calculator Paper — Page 28

1. (a) 54 000 (b) 5 ten thousands, 50 000
2. (a) -7, -1, 0, 5, 13 (b) 20
3. £1.22
4. £1.17
5. (a) 4.95 m
   (b) 4.95 m, 5.02 m, 5.10 m, 5.15 m, 5.20 m
6. (a) 0900 (b) 44 minutes
7. £18.14
8. (a) 0.65 (b) 65%
9. (a) 111 (b) £1.14
10. 2.8 pence
11. (a) 0.7 (b) $\frac{3}{10}$ (c) 7 : 3
12. (a) $4 \times 5 \times 30 = 600$
    (b) 10 times too big.
13. (a) 0.78 (b) 0.3, $\frac{8}{25}$, 33%, $\frac{1}{3}$
14. £281.60
15. Disco's £24
    Bob's £25.50
    Sanjay's £25.85
16. 24.1 kg
17. 5 litres
18. 0.5
19. (a) 474 units
    (b) £55.95
20. USA
    £1.99 cheaper
21. (a) £4800
    (b) £5232
    (c) £900
22. 62.5%
23. (a) (i) 0.9
        (ii) 0.882 352 941
    (b) E.g. $\frac{89}{100}$
24. 0824
25. 0.208569…
    (or 0.21 to 2 d.p.)
26. France. England: $\frac{454}{89} = 5.1$ g/p
    France: $\frac{681}{184} \times 1.58 = 5.8$ g/p
27. 1.094 yards
28. £78.75
29. 12.5%
30. £923.55
31. 889.61 dollars
32. £420
33. (a) 4 (b) 51.2
34. (a) $\sqrt{6.9}$, 2.58, $2\frac{4}{7}$, 1.6^2
    (b) (i) 290 (ii) $\frac{600 \times 30}{80 - 20} = \frac{18\,000}{60} = 300$
35. (a) $2^2 \times 3^3$ (b) 12
36. £1081.57
37. 3150

SECTION 12

Exercise 12 — Page 31

1. £9k
2. $(t + 5)$ years
3. (a) 4q (b) $9x + y$
4. $(3x + 2y)$ pence
5. (a) 6m (b) $m + 2$ (c) m^3
6. (a) 7x (b) $7y - 5$
7. $(4x + 200)$ degrees
8. $(5d + 15)$ pence
9. $7x + 2y$
10. (a) $10a^2$ (b) $6gh$ (c) $2k$ (d) 3
11. (a) $12x$ (b) $12x + 10y$
12. (a) $6x + 5$ (b) $2x + 4$ is twice $x + 2$
13. $(4x + 28)$ cm^2
14.

$a + a$	and	$2a$
$2(a + 1)$	and	$2a + 2$
$2a + 1$	and	$a + a + 1$
a^2	and	$a \times a$

15. (a) (i) $3x + 3$ (ii) $x + 2y$
    (b) (i) $2x + 6$ (ii) $x^2 - x$
    (c) (i) $2x - 5$ (ii) $13 + 3x$
    (d) (i) $2(a - 3)$ (ii) $x(x + 2)$
16. (a) (i) $3x$ (ii) $3a + 2b$ (iii) $3a + 6$
    (b) $8x + 1$
17. (a) £xy (b) £$y(x - 5)$
18. (a) $3ab - 2a - b$ (b) $8x + 19$
19. $(3x - 5)$ years
20. (a) y^5 (b) x^3 (c) z^2
21. (a) $t^5 - t^6$ (b) 30
22. (a) (i) $8 - 6n$ (ii) $4x - 1$
    (b) $p^2 + p - 12$
23. (a) a^4 (b) b^4 (c) c^3 (d) d^4
24. (a) $2(2x + 3)$
    (b) (i) $6y - 9$ (ii) $x^3 - 2x^2$ (iii) $a^2 + ab$
    (c) $x^2 - x$
25. $x^2 - 2x - 24$

123

SECTION 13

Exercise 13 — Page 33

1. (a) 15 (b) 9 (c) 5 (d) 15
2. (a) $x = 5$ (b) $x = 2$ (c) $x = 14$ (d) $x = 7$
3. 6
4.

Input	3	5	−2
Output	9	13	−1

5. (a) 5 (b) 4
6. (a) $x = 10$ (b) $x = 5$ (c) $x = 4$ (d) $x = -6$
7. (a) $x = -1$ (b) $x = \frac{1}{2}$ (c) $x = 5\frac{1}{2}$ (d) $x = -0.8$

SECTION 14

Exercise 14 — Page 34

1. (a) $x = 4$ (b) $x = -1$ (c) $x = 5$ (d) $x = 21$
2. 4
3. $x = 7, \ y = 5, \ z = -3$
4. $x = 6$
5. (a) $x = 11$ (b) $x = 6$
6. (a) $x = 8$ (b) $x = 1$ (c) $x = -4$ (d) $x = 2.5$
7. (a) $p = 5$ (b) $q = -1$ (c) $r = -1\frac{1}{2}$
8. (a) $x = -1.5$ (b) $x = 2.5$ (c) $x = 0.6$ (d) $x = 1.5$
9. (a) $t = 5$ (b) $x = 3\frac{1}{2}$ (c) $y = -6$
10. (a) $n + (n + 3) + (2n - 1) = 4n + 2$
    (b) $4n + 2 = 30, \ n = 7$
11. $n + (2n + 5) = 47, \ 3n + 5 = 47, \ n = 14$. Larger box has 33 chocolates.
12. (a) $(n - 7)$ pence
    (b) $10n + 5(n - 7) = 445, \ n = 32$
        Party hat costs 25 pence.
13. (a) $y = 7$ (b) $p = 2.5$ (c) $t = 3$
14. (a) $a = 1.5$ (b) $b = 4$ (c) $c = 5.6$
15. $x = 5$
16. (a) $x = -21$ (b) $x = 2$ (c) $y = -3.5$ (d) $z = -0.8$
17. (a) $p = 6.5$ (b) $q = 7$
18. (a) (i) $AB = (4d + 3)\,\text{cm}$
        (ii) $CD = (2d + 10)\,\text{cm}$
    (b) (i) $4d + 3 = 2d + 10$
        (ii) $d = 3.5\,\text{cm}$
19. $x = 0.2$
20. $x = 3.9$

SECTION 15

Exercise 15 — Page 36

1. 4
2. −1
3. $P = 40$
4. (a) 2 (b) −8 (c) 8 (d) −15
5. $H = -13$
6. £34
7. $L = -10$
8. $C = 65n$
9. $A = -11$
10. 90
11. 24
12. $T = 100$
13. $P = 15$
14. (a) $m = 0.04w$ (b) 1.2 kg
15. (a) $C = 25x + 10y$ (b) $y = 10$
16. (a) $y = 2x + 1$ (b) $x = 4$
17. (a) £1.05 (b) £1.26
18. (a) 40 km (b) $K = \frac{8M}{5}$ (c) $M = 37.5$
19. $c = 7.2$
20. $t = \frac{c + 5}{3}$
21. $s = -3.75$
22. $m = \frac{n - 3}{p}$
23. $n = 14$
24. $r = \frac{ps}{5}$
25. (a) $v = -7$ (b) $a = \frac{v - u}{t}$

SECTION 16

Exercise 16 — Page 38

1. (a) 21, 25 (b) 30, 26
2. (a) 28, 33 (b) Add 5 to the last term.
   (c) Unit digits of each term must be 3 or 8.
3. (a)
   Pattern number 4
   (b)

Pattern number	1	2	3	4	5	6	7
Number of sticks	3	5	7	9	11	13	15

   (c) (i) 31
       (ii) Double the Pattern number and add 1.
4. (a) 17 (b) 81 (c) $\frac{1}{16}$
5. (a) (i) 30 (ii) Add 6 to the last term.
   (b) Term 12
6. (a) 28, 76 (b) 7, 11
7. 37, 60
8. No. The sequence does not end.
   Sequence: 1, 6, 10, 8, 4, 8, 8, 0, 16, …
9. (a) Pattern 20 has 58 squares.
       $3 \times$ (pattern number) $- 2$ (b) $3n - 2$
10. (a) 19, 23 (b) $4n - 1$
11. (a) $2n + 3$ (b) $4n - 3$
12. (a) 120, 108, 96, 84, 72 (b) $132 - 12n$
13. (a) −3, 0, 5
    (b) Yes. When $n = 8, \ 8^2 - 4 = 60$.

SECTION 17

Exercise 17 — Page 41

1. (a) $R(-6, 2)$, $S(3, -4)$
   (b) $T(-3, 0)$, $U(0, -2)$

2. (a)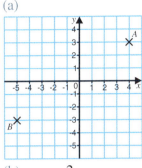
   (b) $p = -2$

3. (a)
   (b) $(5, 2)$

4. (a) Missing entries are: $-5, -2, 1, 4, 7$
   (c) $(0, -2)$

5. (a) Missing entries are: $-3, 1, 3, 5, 7$
   (c) (i) $y = 6$ (ii) $x = -1.75$

6. (a) 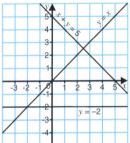   (b) $x + y = 5$

7. (a) $P(0, 3)$, $Q(6, 0)$ (b) $m = 5.5$

8. (a) $y = 3$ (b) $\frac{1}{2}$

9.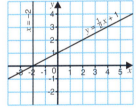

10. (a) Missing entries are: $-6, 3$.
    (b) 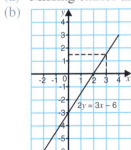   (c) $x = 3$

11. (a) 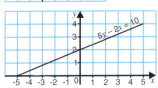   (b) $y = 1.2$

SECTION 18

Exercise 18 — Page 42

1. (a) 8°C   (b) 30 minutes
   (c) 30 minutes

2. (a) 31 miles   (b) 43 km
   (c) Use the graph to convert 100 km to miles and multiply the result by 100. 10 000 km is about 6200 miles.

3. (a)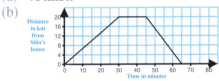
   (b) (i) 54 square feet   (ii) 3 square metres

4. (a) £10   (b) 50 pence

5. (a) 40 km/h
   (b)

6. (a) £480   (b) £100   (c) £980

7. (a) 1306   (b) 1000 and 1100
   (c) 50 km/h

8. (a) 30 minutes   (b) 18 km
   (c) 36 km/h

SECTION 19

Exercise 19 — Page 45

1. (a) $x > 3$ (b) $x \geq -2$
   (c) $x \leq 6$ (d) $x > 2$

2. (a) [number line: closed circle at -2, arrow right]
   (b) [number line: open circle at -3, arrow left]
   (c) [number line: open circle at -1, closed circle at 3]
   (d) [number line: closed circle at -1 arrow left, open circle at 3 arrow right]

3. (a) $x \leq 3$
   (b) [number line: closed circle at 3, arrow left]

4. $-3, -2, -1, 0, 1$

5. $4, 5, 6$

6. (a) $x \leq 2$ (b) $x > 3\frac{1}{2}$ (c) $x < -\frac{4}{3}$

7. (a) $-1, 0, 1, 2$ (b) $1, 2$ (c) $-1, 0, 1$

8. $y > -\frac{3}{5}$

9. (a) $x < 2$ (b) [number line: open circle at 2, arrow left]

SECTION 20

Exercise 20 — Page 46

1. (a) Missing entries are: 7, −1, 2
   (c) $x = \pm 2.2$ (d) $x = \pm 1.4$
2. (b) $y = -2.25$ (c) $x = -2$ or 1
3. (a) Missing entries are: 8, 2, 0, 18
   (b)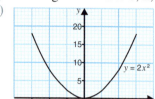
   (c) (i) $y = 12.5$ (ii) $x = \pm 2.45$

Algebra — Non-calculator Paper — Page 47

1. $A(4, 1)$
2. (a) 8 (b) Not an even number.
3. (a) 48 (b) 7
4. 26 points
5. (a)  (b) Missing entry is: 14
   (c) 17 sides
   (d) 35 sides
6. 21
7. (a)   (b) $(-1, 1)$
8. 31, 40
9. (a) $5t$ pence
   (b) $(t + 5)$ pence
10. (a) 10 (b) 4
    (c) 2 (d) 15
11. (a) (i) 30
    (ii) 50th term is an odd number.
    All even terms are odd numbers.
    (b) Add 4 to the last term.
12. (a) **could be even or odd** (b) **always odd**
13. 7
14. $(3x + 5y)$ pence
15. $3a$ and $2a + a$; $2(a - 1)$ and $2a - 2$
16. (a) $5x$ (b) $3a - 4b$ (c) $3m^2$
17. $P = 20$
18. (a) $\frac{1}{2}$ (b) -1
19. (a) $x = -3$ (b) $x = 2.5$
    (c) $x = 6$ (d) $x = 3$
20. (a) Missing entries are: −7, −1, 2, 8
    (c) $x = 2.5$
21. -11
22. (a) (i) $4c$ (ii) $4r - p$
    (b) (i) 27 (ii) 16
23. (a) -5 (b) $2x - 3$
24. $15x - 10$
25. $C = 27n$
26. (a) $(x - 3)$ years (b) $4x$ years
    (c) $x + (x - 3) + 4x = 45$, $x = 8$.
    Louisa 5 years, Hannah 8 years,
    Mother 32 years
27. $3(3x + 4)$
28. (a) $k(k - 2)$ (b) (i) $x = -1$ (ii) $x = \frac{1}{2}$
29. $t = 5$
30. $x = 1.5$
31. $x = 15$
32. $-1, 0, 1$
33. (a)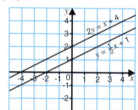
    (b) Lines are parallel, same gradient.
34. (a) $p = \frac{5}{8}$ (b) $W = 60\,\text{kg}$
35. (a) 21, 25 (b) Add 4 to the last term.
    (c) $4n - 3$
36. (a) $x < 2$ (b) $-1, 0, 1$
37. **A**: **Q**, **B**: **S**, **C**: **R**, **D**: **P**
38. (a) p^4 (b) q^4
39. (a) $3n - 5$ (b) $x = \dfrac{y + 5}{2}$
40. (a) Missing entries are: 4, 1
    (c) (i) $x = 1$ (ii) $x = -0.4$ or 2.4
41.
42. (a) $p^2 - 4$ (b) q^6
43. $2x + 3$

Algebra — Calculator Paper — Page 50

1. (a) (i) 22
   (ii) Add the next counting number, 6.
   (b) 12
2. (a) (i) $6y$ (ii) $4m + 1$
   (b) (i) 14 (ii) 8
3. (a) $3x$ pence (b) $(x + 30)$ pence
4. (a) £21.60 (b) £66.60
5. (a) £$(t - 3)$ (b) £$25x$
6. (a) 31, 43
   (b) Add the next even number to the last term.
7. (a) (i) 25 dollars (ii) 18 euros
   (b) From graph, 20 dollars = 24 euros.
   So, 100 dollars = $5 \times 24 = 120$ euros.
8. 24
9. (a) 6 spoonfuls (b) 600 ml
10. (a) $g = 8$ (b) $a = 5$
    (c) $x = 6$ (d) $x = 3$
11. (a) $C = 4u$ (b) $u = 7$
12. (a) 7 (b) $m = 3$ (c) $P = 45$
13. £145.50

14. (a) (i) $3x$ (ii) $3a + 2b$ (iii) $3a + 6$
    (b) $8x + 1$
15. (a) 10 minutes
    (b) Between 10.50 and 11.10.
        Steeper gradient.
    (c) 12 km/h
16. (a) $p = 5$ (b) $q = -\frac{1}{2}$ (c) $y = \frac{1}{4}$
17. (b) $P(-5, -9)$
18. (a) 11 pounds (b) $L = \frac{22K}{10}$ (c) $K = 25$
19. (a) $t^2 - 2t$ (b) $3(y - 4)$
20. (a) (i) $a = 3.5$ (ii) $t = -1$
    (b) $x + x - 3 + x + 7 = 25$
        $3x + 4 = 25, \quad x = 7.$
21. $x = 4.7$
22. (a) (i) x^4 (ii) y^8 (b) $t^2 + 2t - 8$
    (c) $-2, -1, 0, 1, 2, 3$
23. (a) $6n - 1$ (b) 4, 7
24. (a) $80x$ pence (b) $(80r + 60t)$ pence
    (c) (i) $80g + 120 = 1080$ (ii) $g = 12$
25. (a) Missing entries are: $-1, -4, -1$
    (c) $x = \pm 2.2$
26. $x = 4.4$
27. (a) $x = -\frac{1}{5}$ (b) $7x - 3$
    (c) (i) m^6 (ii) n^5
28. (a) $-2, -1, 0, 1$ (b) $m(m + n)$

SECTION 21

Exercise 21 — Page 54

1. (a) CD and EF (b) AB and CD
   (c) (i) $y = 135°$ (ii) **obtuse angle**
2. (a) $\angle ABC = 135°$
   (b)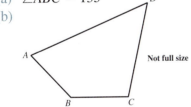
   Not full size
3. (a) $a = 143°$ (supplementary angles)
   (b) $b = 135°$ (angles at a point)
   (c) $c = 48°$ (vertically opposite angles)
       $d = 132°$ (supplementary angles)
       $e = 44°$ ($3e = 132°$, vert. opp. angles)
4. (a) (i) $p = 55°$
       (ii) Vertically opposite angles.
   (b) (i) $q = 125°$
       (ii) p and q are supplementary angles.
5. (a) $\angle PQR = 47°$ (alternate angles)
   (b) $\angle RQS = 68°$
6. $a = 68°$ (supplementary angles)
   $b = 112°$ (corresponding angles)
   $c = 106°$ (allied angles)
7. (a) $a = 117°, \ b = 117°$
   (b) $c = 42°, \ d = 76°, \ e = 62°$
   (c) $f = 51°$

SECTION 22

Exercise 22 — Page 55

1. (a) $a = 27°$ (b) $b = 97°$ (c) $c = 125°$
2. (a) $e = 42°$ (b) $f = 69°$
3. $x = 130°$ ΔPQR is isosceles, $\angle PQR = \angle PRQ$
4. (a) (i) $x = 75°$ (ii) Corres. $\angle$'s, $\angle BDE$
   (b) (i) $y = 50°$ (ii) $55° + 75° + y° = 180°$
5. (a) $x = 64°$ (b) $y = 122°$
7. (a) 9 cm^2 (b) 10 cm^2 (c) 13.5 cm^2
8. (b) (i) $x = 37°$ (ii) acute angle
   (c) 21.66 cm^2
9. 14 cm^2

SECTION 23

Exercise 23 — Page 58

1. (a)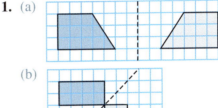
   (b)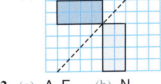
2. (a) A, E (b) N (c) O
3. (a) (i) 3 (ii) 3 (b) (i) 0 (ii) 1
   (c) (i) 0 (ii) 4 (d) (i) 1 (ii) 1
4.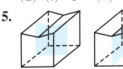
5.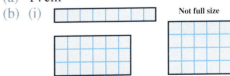
6. **A** and **F**
7. **B** and **D** (SAS)

SECTION 24

Exercise 24 — Page 60

1. (a) 14 cm^2
   (b) (i) Not full size
       (ii) $8 \text{ cm}^2, \ 18 \text{ cm}^2, \ 20 \text{ cm}^2$
2. (a) Square, rhombus (b) Trapezium
   (c) Parallelogram, rhombus
3. (a) $a = 70°$ (b) $b = 132°$
   (c) $c = 110°, \ d = 120°$
4. (a) (i) $x = 78°$ (ii) Supplementary angles
   (b) (i) $y = 130°$
       (ii) Sum of angles in a quad $= 360°$

5. (a) **kite** (b) $\angle ABC = 114°$
7. (a) 30 cm (b) 55.04 cm²
8. 24 cm²
9. (a) $x = 51°$ (b) 40 cm²

SECTION 25

Exercise 25 — Page 61

1. Shape A has rotational symmetry of order 6 and 6 lines of symmetry.
   Shape B has rotational symmetry of order 2 and 2 lines of symmetry.
2. (a) $a = 53°$ (b) $b = 115°$ (c) $c = 140°$
3. (a) $a = 120°$ (b) $b = 60°$, $c = 120°$
   (c) $d = 72°$, $e = 108°$
4. (a) Equilateral
   (b) (i) $x = 60°$ (ii) $y = 120°$
   (c) (i) Rhombus (ii)
5. (a) The shapes cover a surface without overlapping and leaving no gaps.
   (b)
6. (a) $\angle ABC = 144°$ (b) $\angle XCY = 108°$
7. 15 sides
8. $\angle PQX = 151°$
9. Number of sides $= \frac{360°}{30°} = 12$
   Sum of interior angles $= (12 - 2) \times 180°$
   $= 1800°$

SECTION 26

Exercise 26 — Page 63

1. South-East
2. (a) East (b) North-West (c) South-East
3. 26 cm
4. 110°
5. (a) (i) 124° (ii) 304° (b) 6.25 km
7. (b) (i) 250° (ii) 1530 m

SECTION 27

Exercise 27 — Page 66

1. (a) $C = \pi d = 3 \times 10 = 30$ m
   (b) $A = \pi r^2 = 3 \times 5 \times 5 = 75$ m²
2. (a) 15.7 cm (b) 19.6 cm²
3. 225π cm²   8. 1050 cm²
4. 201 cm   9. 106 revolutions
5. 754 cm²   10. (a) 6360 cm² (b) 35 cm
6. 19.9 times   11. 16π cm²
7. 81.7 m²   12. 796 cm²
13. Yes. Semi-circle $= \frac{1}{2} (\pi \times 10^2) = 50\pi$ cm²
    Circle $= \pi \times 5^2 = 25\pi$ cm²

SECTION 28

Exercise 28 — Page 68

1. (a) 5 faces, 8 edges, 5 vertices (b) **R**
2. (a) (b)
3. (a) 22 cm (b) 11 cm²
   (c)
4. 37 m²
5. (a) 30 cubes
   (b) (i)
   (ii) 62 cm²
6. (a) C. A $= 24$ cm³
          B $= 24$ cm³
          C $= 27$ cm³
   (b) (i)
   (ii) 52 cm²
   (c) **B**: 56 cm²
7. (a) 24 m³
   (b) 68 m²
8. 2.58 m²
9. 2.5 cm
10. 1530 cm³
11. (a) 414 cm²
    (b) 405 cm³
12. $AB = 3.5$ cm
13. (a)
    (b)
14. 26.7 cm³
15. (a) 36.9 m²
    (b) 295.2 m³
    (c) 32 cm
16. 352 cm²
17. (a) 32 673 cm²
    (b) 20.1 cm

SECTION 29

Exercise 29 — Page 72

1.
2. (a) (b) 36 cm
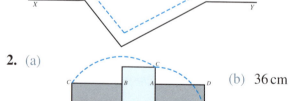
3. (a) (b) 8.4 km

4. (a) (b) 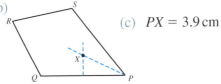 (c) $PX = 3.9\,\text{cm}$

SECTION 30

Exercise 30 — Page 74

1. (a) 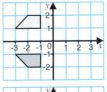 (b)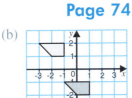

(c)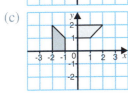

2. (a) Rotation, 90° anticlockwise, about (0, 0).
(b) Translation 4 units to the right and 3 units down $\left(\text{or}\begin{pmatrix}4\\-3\end{pmatrix}\right)$.
(c) Reflection in $y = 3$.

3.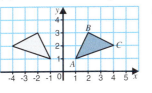

4.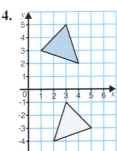

5. (a) Reflection in $x = 0$ (y axis).
(b) Rotation, 90° clockwise, about (0, 0).

6. (a) $x = -1$
(b) One unit to the left and 2 units up.
(c)

7. (a) Shape D has coordinates: (0, 0), (0, −2), (3, 0).
(b) Rotation, through 180°, about (0, 1).

8. (a) Reflection in $x = 3$.
(b) Rotation, through 180°, about (2, 1).
(c) Translation $\begin{pmatrix}2\\-3\end{pmatrix}$.

9. Reflection in $y = x$.

10. (a) Translation $\begin{pmatrix}3\\2\end{pmatrix}$.
(b)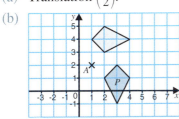

SECTION 31

Exercise 31 — Page 77

1.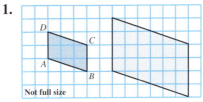

2. Enlargement, scale factor 3, centre (0, 0).
3. (a) Centre (0, 2), scale factor 2.
(b) Coordinates of enlarged shape: (3, 2), (3, 4), (1, 4), (−1, 0).

4.   **5.**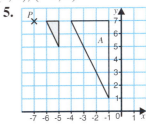

6. (a) Ratio of widths $= 1 : 2$ **but** ratio of lengths $= 5 : 7$.
(b) 7.5 cm
7. (a) $PQ = 3.75\,\text{cm}$ (b) $AC = 5.2\,\text{cm}$

SECTION 32

Exercise 32 — Page 78

1. $BC = 13\,\text{cm}$
2. $PQ = 8\,\text{m}$
3. 28.7 cm
4. 8.94 units
5. $QR = 7.48\,\text{cm}$
area $\Delta PQR = 18.7\,\text{cm}^2$
6. $AD = 17.7\,\text{cm}$
7. (a) $13\,\text{cm}^2$
(b) $AB = 5.4\,\text{cm}$
8. 45.6 cm
9. $AE = 5.7\,\text{cm}$

SECTION 33

Exercise 33 — Page 81

1. (a) 15 grams   (b) 3.28 kg
(c) 44 km/h
2. (a) Metres   (b) Litres
(c) Square metres   (d) Grams
3. 14 m
4. (a) 4000 m   (b) 2.5 miles
5. 54 litres
6. 8 pounds
7. (a) $1.35\,\text{m}^2$ (b) $200\,000\,\text{cm}^3$
8. £813
9. 165 mm
10. (a) $d = 91.5\,\text{km}$
(b) $9.15\,\text{km} \leq d < 92.5\,\text{km}$
11. (a) πr^2 and $2bh$ (b) πr^3 and $b^2 h$

Shape, Space, Measures

Non-calculator Paper — Page 82

1. (a) (b)
2. (a) 5.6 cm (b) (i) 106° (ii) Obtuse
3. (a) 12 (b) 5 (c) cone
4. (a) 17 cm² (b) 24 cm
5. (a) East (b) South-West
6. (a) 12 cm³
   (b) (i) 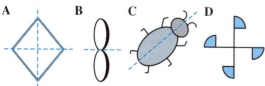 (ii)
7. (a) $a = 58°$ (vertically opposite angles)
   (b) $b = 155°$ (supplementary angles)
   (c) $c = 150°$ (angles at a point)
8. (a) (i)
   A   B   C   D
   (ii) Place a mirror on the dotted line to see if the reflection is the same as the actual image.
   (b) (i) **TRUE** (ii) **FALSE**
       (iii) **FALSE** (iv) **TRUE**
9. (a)
10. (a) $a = 67°$ Angles in a triangle add to 180°.
    (b) $b = 54°$ Isosceles Δ.
        $b = 180° − (2 × 63°)$
    (c) $c = 126°$ Angles in a quadrilateral add to 360°.
        $c = 180° − (360° − 306°)$
11. (a)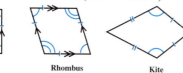
        Square   Rhombus   Kite
    (b) Square, rectangle (c) Square
12. 32 km
13. 25 litres
14. (a) 18 cm² (b) 25 cm²
15.
16. (a) 72° (b) 85.6 cm²

17. (a) (i) $p = 52$ (ii) $q = 76$
    (b) Alternate angles
18. (a) (i) 5 cm (ii) 100 km
    (b) (i) 060° (ii) 240°
19.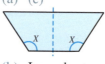
20. $BC = 13$ cm
21. 14π cm
22. (a) 125 cm
    (b) 40 cm
    (c) 140°
    (d) 118.5 cm
23. (a) abc has dimension 3 (volume)
    (b) πa and $\sqrt{a^2 - c^2}$ and $2(a + b + c)$
24. 45 cm³

Shape, Space, Measures

Calculator Paper — Page 85

1. (a) 5.8 cm
2. (a) 8000 g and 8 kg (b) 0.2 km (c) 1.4 kg
3. (a) (c)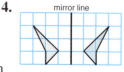
   (b) Isosceles trapezium
4.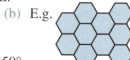
5. (a) $A(2, 3)$ (b) $C(-2, -1)$ (c) $D(-2, 3)$
6. **A** and **G**, **C** and **E**.
7. (a) Hexagon (b) E.g.
8. $230° + 120° = 350°$
   Angles at a point should total 360°.
9. Height 175 cm, weight 70 kg
10. (a) Reflection in the line $x = 5$.
    (b) Rotation, 90° anticlockwise, about (0, 0).
    (c) Translation $\begin{pmatrix} 4 \\ 1 \end{pmatrix}$
11. (a) $a = 40°, b = 95°, c = 135°$ (b) $d = 40°$
12. (a) (b)
13. (a) (i) (ii) 46 cm²
    (b) 2.5 cm
14. (a) $x = 3$
    (b) Shape B has vertices at:
        (6, 2), (8, 6), (6, 8), (4, 6).
15. (a) 4 (b) 1
16. 40.2 cm
17. 864 boxes
18. 297 m²
19.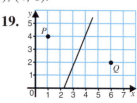

20. (a) Ext. $\angle = \frac{360°}{6} = 60°$.
    $a =$ int. $\angle = 180° - 60° = 120°$
    (b) $b = 15°$
21. $754\,\text{cm}^3$
22. (a) $2.6\,\text{m}^2$ (b) $3.9\,\text{m}^3$
23. (b) (i) $215°$ (ii) $17\,\text{km}$
24.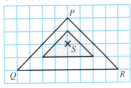
25. $28.3\,\text{km}$
26. (a) $70.5\,\text{km}$ (b) $69.5\,\text{km}$

SECTION 34

Exercise 34 Page 88

1. (a) (i) E.g.

Gender	Mode of transport
M	Bus
F	Cycle

   (b) Data will be biased, as people at bus station are likely to travel by bus.

2. (a) Laila (b) Ria
   (c) Corrin.
       Pupils are in the same class and June is a later month in the school year than the other months given.

3. E.g.

Resort	Tally
Cervinia	|||| ||
Livigno	|||| ||
Tonale	|||| ||||

4. (a) E.g. May play a different sport. May play more than one of these sports. Answer does not indicate which sport is played.
   (b) Which sport(s) do you play?
       Football ☐ Rugby ☐ Hockey ☐
       Netball ☐ Swimming ☐ Tennis ☐
       Other ☐ (state) ……… None ☐

5. (a)

Weight (w kg)	Tally	Frequency
$30 \leq w < 40$	||||	4
$40 \leq w < 50$	|||| ||	7
$50 \leq w < 60$	|||| ||	7
$60 \leq w < 70$	|||| |||	8
$70 \leq w < 80$	|	1
$80 \leq w < 90$	|||	3

   (b) $60 \leq w < 70$

6. (a)

	Theatre	Art gallery	Science museum	Totals
Girls	11	9	7	27
Boys	8	2	13	23
Totals	19	11	20	50

   (b) 7

7. (a) (b)

	French	German	Spanish
Boys	23		
Girls			

8. (a) (i) Too personal.
       (ii) In which age group are you?
            Under 16 ☐ 16 to 19 ☐ Over 19 ☐
   (b) (i) Only students already using the library are sampled.
       (ii) Give to students as they enter (or leave) the college.

9. E.g. Please give the reason why you no longer attend the Youth Centre.
   Unsuitable opening hours ☐
   Attend new Sports Centre ☐
   Bullying ☐
   Other (please state) ……………

10. E.g. Two thirds of men were over 45.
    All women are aged 16 to 45.
    Twice as many women as men.

11. No.
    Men: $\frac{180}{200} = 90\%$ Women: $\frac{240}{300} = 80\%$
    Higher proportion of men can drive.

12. (a) 2
    (b) Yes. 21 people have cats **and** 17 people have dogs.
    (c) 25 dogs

SECTION 35

Exercise 35 Page 91

1. (a) (i) 60 (ii) 80
   (b)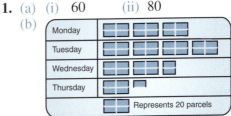
       Represents 20 parcels

2. (a) Cola (b) 7 (c) 32
3. (a) 8 (b) 16% (c)

Strawberry	👤 👤
Vanilla	👤
Other	👤 👤 👤

   👤 = 5 people

5. (a) Range: 2, mode: 2
   (b) Women's team had a larger range (5) and higher mode (3).

SECTION 36

Exercise 36 — Page 94

1. (a) 7 cm (b) 10 cm (c) 11 cm (d) 11.3 cm
2. (a) £9 (b) £10.50 (c) £11.50
   (d) Median.
   Mode is the lowest price and mean is affected by the one higher-priced meal.
3. (a) 29 (b) 9 (c) 6 (d) 8 (e) 6
4. (a) (i) 4.9 hours (ii) 6 hours
   (b) Much bigger variation in the number of hours of sunshine each day and lower average.
5. 38 points
6. (a) 5 (b) 9
   (c) Reg: mean;   Reg 9, Helen 8.6
   Helen: mode;   Reg 9, Helen 10
   Friend: median; Reg 9, Helen 9
7. (a) (i) 1 (ii) 3 (iii) 3.35
   (b) Mode **and** median
8. (a) 11 to 15 (b) 16.4
9. 29 minutes

SECTION 37

Exercise 37 — Page 96

1. (a) 12 (b) 22°C (c) 14°C
   (d) 5°C or 24°C.
   Temperature can be either 2°C above previous maximum, or 2°C below previous minimum.
2. (a) £720 (b) £240
3. (a) $\frac{5}{18}$ (b) 72 students
4.

Country	USA	France	Spain	Greece
Angle	126°	90°	99°	45°

5. (a) 1 | 0 means 10 text messages

   ```
   0 | 2 3 5 5 7 9
   1 | 0 1 2 3 5 7
   2 | 0 1
   ```
   (b) 19
6. (a) 108° (b) £15 750
7. (a) Boys | Girls   2 | 5 means 2.5 cm
   ```
                 | 2 | 5
             5 5 | 3 | 0 5 5 5
       5 5 5 5 0 0 | 4 | 0 5 5
               0 0 | 5 | 0 5
   ```
   (b) Girls have more variation in their estimates than boys: Girls 3.0 cm, Boys 1.5 cm.

SECTION 38

Exercise 38 — Page 99

1. (a)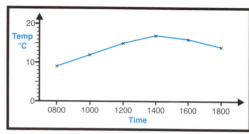
   (b) 8°C
   (c) (i) 16°C
       (ii) Actual temperatures are only known at times when readings are taken.
2. (a)

Weight (w grams)	Tally	Frequency
$490 \leq w < 495$	‖	2
$495 \leq w < 500$	⋕ ⋕ ‖	11
$500 \leq w < 505$	⋕ ‖	6
$505 \leq w < 510$	⋕ ‖‖	8
$510 \leq w < 515$	‖‖	3

   (c) $495 \leq w < 500$
3. (b) $10 \leq d < 15$ (c) 10%
4. Vertical scale is not uniform.
5. (b) $175 \leq h < 180$
6. (a) $80 \leq age < 90$
   (b) 40
   (c) (ii) Women:

Age (a years)	Frequency
$60 \leq a < 70$	1
$70 \leq a < 80$	5
$80 \leq a < 90$	13
$90 \leq a < 100$	6

   (iii) More men under 80 than women. Only women aged over 90. Women have greater range of ages.
7. (a) 7 (b) 3 (c) 67

SECTION 39

Exercise 39 — Page 101

1. (b) Negative correlation. As engine size increases, the time taken to travel 500 m decreases.
   (c) 16 to 17 seconds
2. (a) (i) **C** (ii) **A** (iii) **B** (b) **C**
3. (a) 36 (b) 60 (c) No
   (d) Yes (e) Positive

4. (b) Negative correlation.
   As temperature increases, the time taken for a 2 cm ice cube to melt decreases.
   (d) 50 minutes   (e) 24.5°C
   (f) At 35°C the line of best fit gives a time less than zero, which is impossible.

SECTION 40

Exercise 40 — Page 104

1. (a) C   (b) B
2.
3. (a) $\frac{1}{8}$ (b) $\frac{4}{8} = \frac{1}{2}$ (c) $\frac{5}{8}$
4. (a)

Ways to score a total of 6.	
Number on red dice	Number on blue dice
1	5
2	4
3	3
4	2
5	1

   (b) Total score of 6. There are five ways to score a total of 6, but only one way to score a total of 12, i.e. (Red 6) + (Blue 6).
5. 0.14
6. (a) 0.1   (b) 0.7
7. (a)

	France	Germany	Spain	Total
Female	2	23	9	34
Male	15	2	9	26
Total	17	25	18	60

   (b) $\frac{25}{60} = \frac{5}{12}$
8. (a)

Second spinner

		2	3	4	5
First spinner	1	1	2	3	4
	1	1	2	3	4
	2	0	1	2	3
	3	1	0	1	2

   (b) 1   (c) $\frac{5}{16}$
9. (a) $\frac{2}{5}$ (b) 0.6
10. (a) $\frac{9}{20} = 0.45$
    (b) 2, 3, 3, 4, 5. Numbers 2, 3, 4, 5 have occurred and 3 has occurred twice as often as other numbers.
    (c) 100. Relative frequency of 5 is $\frac{1}{5}$.
    $\frac{1}{5} \times 500 = 100$
11. (a) HHH, HHT, HTH, THH, THT, HTT, TTH, TTT   (b) $\frac{3}{8}$
12. (a) $\frac{5}{8}$ (b) $\frac{7}{8}$

Handling Data — Section Review

Non-calculator Paper — Page 106

1. (a) 4   (b) 11   (c) 22
2. (a) (i) Blue
       (ii) Blue has only one sector. Red has seven sectors and Black has four sectors.
   (b)
   (c) $\frac{1}{12}$
3. (a) Spain   (b) 12   (c) 51
4. (a) 3   (b) 4   (c) 6   (d) 5
5. (a) 3   (b) 30   (c) 60
6. (a) (i)

Pantomime	Angle
Aladdin	135°
Cinderella	105°
Jack and the Bean Stalk	75°
Peter Pan	45°

   (ii) Aladdin
   (b) (i) 72   (ii) $33\frac{1}{3}\%$
7. (a)

×	1	2	3	4
1	1	2	3	4
2	2	4	6	8
3	3	6	9	12

   (b) $\frac{2}{12} = \frac{1}{6}$
   (c) $\frac{4}{12} = \frac{1}{3}$
8. (a) A: Tuff hatchback
       B: Ace supermini
       C: Nippy sports
       D: Mega estate
   (b) Nippy sports
9. 7.6
10. E.g. Leading question.
    Question has more than one part.
11. (a)

	4│5 means 4.5 cm
4	5 8 8
5	0 0 4 4 5 8
6	0 2 4 5 5 5 6 8
7	0 2 4

   (b) 2.9 cm
12. (a) $\frac{17}{75}$
    (b) Yes. Female: $\frac{12}{50} = 24\%$
        Male: $\frac{5}{25} = 20\%$
13. (a) 1   (b) 2   (c) 2.2
14. (a) 0.7   (b) 0.44

Handling Data

Calculator Paper — Page 109

1. (a) 170
   (b)
Day	Books
Monday	📖📖📖📖📖
Tuesday	📖📖📖📖📖📖
Wednesday	📖📖📖📖
Thursday	📖📖
Friday	📖📖📖📖📖📖📖

   📖 = 10 books

2. (a)
Number of people in boat	Tally	Frequency
1					3
2	⩘ ||	7
3					3
4	⩘	5
5				2

   (b) 2 (c) 7.4

3. (a) (i) **TRUE** (ii) **FALSE** (iii) **TRUE**
   (b) Conduct traffic surveys outside schools in different locations at the same time of day, for the same period of time, on the same day.

4. 0.91

5. (a) X1, X2, X3, Y1, Y2, Y3
   (b) $\frac{4}{6} = \frac{2}{3}$

6. (a) $\frac{1}{2}$ (b) In a small number of trials there will be differences in the number of heads and tails that occur.

7. (a) 20 (b) 6 (c) 5
   (d)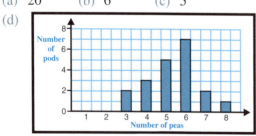

8. (a) 15 (b) 28 g (c) 30 g (d) 29.3 g

9. Vertical scale does not begin at zero, so, improvements are exaggerated.

10. (a) $\frac{3}{20}$ (b) $\frac{7}{20}$

11. E.g.
Method of travel	Tally
Bus	
Car	

12.
Region	Midlands	London	Southern England	Northern England
Frequency	88°	144°	32°	96°

13. (b) Positive correlation. Taller men tend to have a better best jump than shorter men.
    (d) (i) 1.68 m (ii) 5.7 m

14. 1.8

15. E.g. Ask what foods they ate **today** in the school canteen. Give choices to tick.

16. (b) 65 g (c) $60 \leq w < 80$

17. (a) 0.3 (b) 175

Exam Practice

Non-calculator Paper — Page 112

1. (a) Six thousand seven hundred and forty
   (b) 7 hundreds, 700

2. (a) 3 (b)
Day	Cars
Monday	⊕⊕
Tuesday	⊕⊕⊕
Wednesday	⊕◐
Thursday	⊕⊕◁
Friday	⊕⊕◐

   ⊕ = 4 cars

3. (a) 7, 19, 30, 105, 2002
   (b) (i) 75 (ii) 133 (iii) 286

4. (a) 7, 12, 17 (b) 91, 82, 73

5. (a) (i) 4 (ii) 27 (iii) 64
   (b) 13 and 27

6. (a) Shade any 12 squares.
   (b) (i) 0.6 (ii) 60%
   (c) (i) **31 302** (ii) 14 000
   (d) $100 \times 60 = 6000$

7. (a) West (b) North-West

8. (a) $5d$ pence (b) $(d + 25)$ pence

9. (b) $(3, -2)$

10. $P = 26$

11. (a) (i) 2 (ii) 1 (b) 16 cm (c) 8 cm^2

12. (a) £37 (b) 15 days

13. (a) 20 miles (b) 24 km

14. (a) 43 914 (b) 30.5

15. (a) 3 (b) 4 (c) number line with X at position between $\frac{1}{2}$ and 1 (labels 0, $\frac{1}{2}$, 1)

16. A: 4, B: 2, C: 2

17. (a) 10 degrees (b) $-3°C$

18. (a) $\frac{1}{2}$ (b) $\frac{7}{20}$

19. 1.05 pm

20. (a) (i) $a = 145°$
    (ii) Supp. ∠'s, $a + 35° = 180°$.
    (b) (i) $b = 83°$
    (ii) Angles in triangle sum to 180°.
    (c) (i) $c = 35°$
    (ii) Vertically opposite angles.

21. (a) (i) 3.28 (ii) 5.4 (iii) 35
    (b) 31
22. (a) (i) $7a$ (ii) $11y - x$ (iii) $3a^2$
    (b) (i) $x = 3$ (ii) $x = 4$ (iii) $x = 3$
    (c) 5
23. (a) 25% (b) 90
24. 60 km/h
25. (a) 0.78 (b) 0.3, $\frac{8}{25}$, 33%, $\frac{1}{3}$
    (c) (i) $1\frac{1}{9}$ (ii) $\frac{3}{20}$
26. (a) 34
    (b) 25
27. (a) 10
    (b) 1 : 6
28. (a) 22 pounds
    (b) £2.99
29. (a)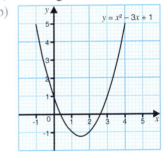
    (b) (1, 2)
30. (a) $x + (2x - 1) + 3x = 41$
    (b) $x = 7$. Numbers on cards: 7, 13, 21
31. (a) 4.128 (b) 41 280
32. 12π m
33. (a) $x = 2$ (b) $y = 9$
34. (a) (i) $2^4 \times 3$ (ii) $2^2 \times 3^3$ (b) 432
35. Greatest: 11.5 kg, least: 10.5 kg
36. $3n - 1$
37. (a) Enlargement, scale factor $\frac{1}{2}$, centre (0, 1)
    (b) Rotation, 90° anticlockwise, about (1, −1)
38. (a) $\frac{5}{22}$ (b) $\frac{7}{22}$ (c) $\frac{9}{22}$
39. (a) Missing entries are: 5, −1, 1
    (b)
    (c) $y = -1.25$
    (d) $x = 0.4$ or $x = 2.6$
40. $V = 3 \times 4 \times 4 \times 8 = 384 \text{ cm}^3$
41. (a) (i) $5(a - 2)$ (ii) $x(x - 6)$
    (b) (i) $8a + 2$ (ii) $x^2 - 6x + 8$
    (c) $t = \frac{W - 3}{5}$ (d) m^5
42. $\sqrt{a^2 + b^2}$ and $4(a + b + c)$
    Both have dimension 1.
43. $-1 < x \leq 2$

Exam Practice
Calculator Paper — Page 116

1. (a) 5 (b) 3570 (c) Four tenths
2. (a) −7, −1, 0, 5, 13 (b) 20
3.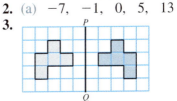
4. £2.78
5. (a) Pattern number 4
   (b)
Pattern number	1	2	3	4	5
Number of matchsticks	5	9	13	17	21
   (c) Pattern number 10
   (d) (i) 401
       (ii) Multiply the Pattern number by 4 and add 1.
6. £205
7. (a) Metres (b) 12 m
8. 20
9. **A** and **D**
10. 684 dollars
11. (a) 53 minutes (b) 0739
12. Turns through 180° in a clockwise direction.
13. (a) $x = 6$ (b) $x = 3$
14. £670.40
15. (a) −9 (b) 5 (c) $3(x - 2)$
16. £281.60
17. −114.3
18. (a) 36 (b) 12.5%
19. 80%, $\frac{7}{8}$, $\frac{8}{9}$, 0.9
20. $P = 36$
21. 58.8 kg
22. $a = 62°$, $b = 60°$, $c = 135°$
23. (a) 56.5 cm (b) 201 cm²
24. $\frac{1}{15}$
25. (a) 60 cm (b) $d = \frac{a + b}{3}$
26. (a) (i) $6x + 4y$ (ii) $3pq$ (b) $3(t - 4)$
27. (a) 0815
    (b) (i) Between 0820 and 0835. Steepest gradient.
        (ii) 12 km/h
28. (b) Negative correlation.
        Countries with higher birth rates tend to have a lower life expectancy.
    (d) 52 to 57
29. $x = 20$
30. 80
31. (b) 2.15 km, 295°
32. (a) $y = 7$ (b) $p = 2.5$
    (c) $t = 3$
33. (a) 700 cm³ (b) 13.51 kg
34. $x = 3.8$
35. (a) 30 (b) $2 \leq t < 3$
    (c) 2.07 hours
36. £14.40
37. 61.1%
38. 0.45, correct to 2 s.f.
    All numbers in question given to 3 s.f., so, answer can only be correct to 2 s.f.

Index

12-hour clock 17
24-hour clock 17
3-dimensional shapes . . . 57, 67, 68
3-figure bearings 63

a

accuracy 5, 80
accurate drawing 55, 59, 71
acute angle 53
acute-angled triangle 55
adding algebraic terms 31
addition 1, 3, 8, 10, 31
addition of decimals 3
addition of fractions 10
addition of negative numbers . . . 8
algebra . . 31, 33, 34, 36, 38, 45, 46
algebraic expressions 31, 36
allied angles 53
alternate angles 53
angle bisector 71
angles 53, 55, 63
angles at a point 53
approximation 5
arc 65
area 55, 59, 65, 67, 68, 80
area of a circle 65
area of a triangle 55
ascending order 1
average speed 23
averages 93, 94
axes of symmetry 57

b

back to back stem and leaf
  diagrams 96
balance method 33
bar charts 91
bar-line graphs 91
basic hourly rate of pay 19
bearings 63
'best buy' 17
biased results 88
bisector of an angle 71
brackets 31, 34

c

cancelling fractions 10
capacity 80
centre of enlargement 76
centre of rotation 73
changing decimals to fractions . . 3
changing decimals to
  percentages 15

changing fractions to decimals . . 10
changing fractions to
  percentages 15
changing percentages to
  decimals 15
changing percentages to
  fractions 15
changing the subject of
  a formula 36
changing units 80
checking answers 5
chord 65
circle 65, 68
circumference 65
circumference of a circle 65
class intervals 88
classes 88
collecting data 88
combinations of shapes 67
combinations of transformations . 73
common difference 38
common factors 12
comparing data 91, 93, 94
comparing distributions . 91, 93, 94
compass points 63
compasses 55, 59, 71
complementary angles 53
compound measures 23
compound shapes 67
congruent shapes 57
congruent triangles 57
constructions 55, 59, 63, 71
continuing a sequence 38
continuous data 88, 98
continuous measures 88
conversion graph 42
converting units of
  measurement 80
coordinates 40
correlation 101
corresponding angles 53
cube 67
cube number 13
cube roots 13
cuboid 57, 67, 68
cylinder 68

d

data 88
data collection sheets 88
databases 88
decimal places 3, 5
decimal point 3
decimals 3, 5, 10, 15
degree of accuracy 5

degrees 53
denominator 10
density 23
descending order 1
diameter 65
dimensions 80
direct proportion 21
direction 63
discrete data 88
discrete measures 88
distance-time graphs 42
dividing algebraic expressions . . 31
dividing by 10, 100, 1000 1
dividing by multiples of 10 1
dividing decimals 3
dividing decimals by
  powers of 10 3
division 1, 3, 8, 10, 13, 31
division of fractions 10
division of negative numbers . . . 8
double inequalities 45
drawing angles 53, 63
drawing solid shapes 67
drawing triangles 55

e

edges 67
elevations 67
enlargement 76
enlarging shapes 76
equally likely outcomes 103
equation of a straight line 40
equations 33, 34, 40, 46
equidistant 71
equilateral triangle 55
equivalent fractions 10
equivalent ratios 21
estimate of mean 93
estimating probability 103
estimating quantities 80
estimation 5
events 103
exchange rates 17
expanding brackets 31, 34
expressions 31, 36
exterior angle of a triangle 55
exterior angles 55, 61
exterior angles of a
  regular polygon 61

f

faces 67
factorising 31
factors 12, 31

foreign currency 17
forming equations 34, 36
formulae 36, 80
fractional scale factors 76
fractions 3, 10, 15
frequency 88, 91
frequency distribution 88, 93
frequency distribution
 tables 88, 93
frequency polygons 98
frequency tables 88
function 40

g

gradient 40, 42
graphical solution of
 equations 40, 46
graphs 40, 42, 46
greater than or equal to, $\geq$ 45
greater than, $>$ 45
grouped data 88, 93, 98
grouped frequency
 distribution 88, 93, 98
groups 88, 93

h

hexagon 61
highest common factor 12
histograms 98
hourly rate of pay 19
household bills 19
hypotenuse 78
hypothesis 88

i

image 73
imperial units of measurement . . 80
improper fractions 10
income tax 19
index form 12, 13
indices 12, 13
inequalities 45
intercept 40
interest 19
interior angles of a polygon 61
isometric drawings 67
isosceles trapezium 59
isosceles triangle 55

k

kite 59

l

large numbers 13
least common multiple 12
length 80
less than or equal to, $\leq$ 45
less than, $<$ 45
linear function 40
line graphs 98
line of best fit 101
line of symmetry 57
line segments 53
linear sequence 38
listing outcomes 104
loci 71
locus 71
long division 1
long multiplication 1

m

making 3-dimensional shapes . . 67
maps 63
mass 23, 80
maximum value 46
mean 93, 94
measurement 5, 80
measuring angles 53, 63
median 93, 94
metric units of measurement . . . 80
midpoint of a class 93
minimum value 46
mirror line 73
misleading graphs 98
mixed numbers 10
mode 91, 93, 94, 96
money 3, 17, 19
multiples 12
multiplication 1, 3, 8, 10, 31
multiplication of fractions 10
multiplication of
 negative numbers 8
multiplying algebraic
 expressions 31
multiplying by
 10, 100, 1000, … 1
multiplying by
 multiples of 10 1
multiplying decimals 3
multiplying decimals by
 powers of 10 3
multiplication tables 1
mutually exclusive events 103

n

negative correlation 101
negative numbers 8
nets 67
n th term of a sequence 38
number line 8, 45
number patterns 38
number sequences 38
numbers 1, 3, 8, 12, 38
numerator 10

o

obtuse angle 53
obtuse-angled triangle 55
octagon 61
order of operations 1
order of rotational symmetry . . . 57
ordering decimals 3
ordering numbers 1, 8
outcomes 103, 104
overtime rate of pay 19

p

π 65
parallel lines 53
parallelogram 59
pay 19
pentagon 61
per cent 15
percentage change 15
percentage decrease 15
percentage increase 15
percentages 15, 17, 19
perfect correlation 101
perimeter 55, 59
perpendicular bisector of a line . 71
perpendicular from
 a point on a line 71
perpendicular from
 a point to a line 71
perpendicular height 55
perpendicular lines 53
personal finance 19
pictogram 91
pie charts 96
place value 1, 3
planes of symmetry 57
plans 67
polygon 61
population density 23
positive correlation 101
possibility space diagram 104
power form 12
powers 12, 13, 31
primary data 88
prime factors 12
prime numbers 12
prism 68
probability 103, 104
probability experiments 103
probability scale 103
product of prime factors 12
proportion 21
protractor 53, 55, 59
Pythagoras' Theorem 78

q

quadratic equations 46
quadratic function 46
quadrilateral 59, 61
qualitative data 88
quantitative data 88
questionnaires 88

r

radius 65
random events 103
range 91, 93
ratio 21
reading numbers 1
reading scales 80
rearranging formulae 36
reciprocals 13
rectangle 59, 67
recurring decimals 10
reflection 73
reflex angle 53
regular polygon 61
regular tessellations 61
relative frequency 103
removing brackets:
 by expanding 31, 34
rhombus 59
right angle 53
right-angled triangle 55, 78
rotation 73
rotational symmetry 57
rounding 5
rules of indices 13, 31

s

sample 88
savings 19
scale drawing 63
scale factor 76
scalene triangle 55
scales on maps and plans 63
scatter graphs 101
secondary data 88
sector 65
segment 65
sequences of numbers 38
shapes . . 55, 57, 59, 61, 65, 67, 68
sharing in a given ratio 21
short division 1
short multiplication 1
significant figures 5
similar figures 76
Simple Interest 19
simplifying expressions 31
simplifying fractions 10
simplifying ratios 21

sketch diagrams 55
slope 40
small numbers 13
solid shapes 67, 68
solving equations 33, 34, 40
solving equations by
 trial and improvement 34
solving equations by
 working backwards 33
solving equations graphically . . 46
solving equations:
 by inspection 33
solving equations:
 using the balance method . . . 33
solving inequalities 45
solving quadratic equations 46
speed 23, 42
spread 93
square 59, 61, 67
square numbers 12, 38
square roots 12
standard index form 13
statistical bias 88
statistical diagrams 91, 96,
 98, 101
stem and leaf diagrams 96
straight line graph 40
subject of a formula 36
substituting 36, 40
subtracting algebraic terms 31
subtraction 1, 3, 8, 10, 31
subtraction of decimals 3
subtraction of fractions 10
subtraction of negative numbers . 8
sum of angles in a triangle 55
sum of the angles of
 a quadrilateral 59
sum of the exterior angles of
 a polygon 61
sum of the interior angles of
 a polygon 61
supplementary angles 53
surface area 67, 68
symmetrical 57
symmetry 57

t

table of values 40, 46
tally marks 88
tangent 65
tax 19
taxable income 19
tax allowance 19
temperature 8
terms 31
terms of a sequence 38
tessellations 61
Theorem of Pythagoras 78

three-dimensional
 shapes 57, 67, 68
three-figure bearings 63
time 17
time series 98
timetables 17
'top heavy' fractions 10
transformations 73
translation 73
transversal 53
trapezium 59
trend 98, 101
trial and improvement 12, 34
trials 103
triangle 55, 57, 61, 67, 78
triangular numbers 38
two-dimensional drawing of
 3-dimensional shapes 67
two-way tables 88
types of triangle 55

u

unitary method of sharing 21
units of measurement 80
using a calculator 5, 12, 13
using formulae 36

v

VAT 17
variables (statistical) 88
vector 73
vertex 53
vertically opposite angles 53
vertices 67
volume 23, 67, 68, 80

w

wages 19
whole numbers 1, 5
writing equations 34
writing numbers 1

x

x coordinate 40

y

$y = mx + c$ 40
y coordinate 40

z

zero correlation 101